Honored Burden

Howard Calhoun

ISBN 978-1-0980-7889-8 (paperback)
ISBN 978-1-0980-7890-4 (digital)

Christian Faith Publishing, Inc.
832 Park Avenue
Meadville, PA 16335
www.christianfaithpublishing.com

Printed in the United States of America

Dedicated to my father and mother and in appreciation
of my brothers and sisters for always giving their best

Preface

I was once told by a book reviewer that my book offered a limited view of society and, therefore, would be relevant to a limited readership locally, perhaps regionally at best. I recognize the truth as more adequately stated as a lesser limit because every book has its limits. I dispute relevancy the same as I quarrel with the importance of small businesses' value beyond its local or regional market. Small businesses contribute greatly to the world economy.

The tapestry of a society is illuminated when it includes the fabrics derived from some of the most rural and backwoods communities as part of the story. To exclude or qualify such contributions as minimally important is dismissive and elitist. It says more about the broader narrative of why so many stories never see the light of day. Untold stories rob society of important histories. Perhaps it goes even deeper. When a society, for whatever reason, decides a demographic is insignificant, its treatment of that demographic is to depress and exclude.

Many early slaveholders believed education was wasted on slaves. By withholding education as a standard practice, it robbed the individuals of their potential talents and skills that would serve those individuals and their succeeding generations. Also, it would have served and uplifted those who held them captive. Both groups lose when individuals are not allowed to pursue their greatest potential.

When society's values are told by a select few based on a capricious and privileged list of demographics, it prejudges and defines significance and relevancy from a single perspective. It proceeds along a specific rationalization with a targeted agenda. That agenda is then projected onto a global audience as an unbiased universal truth. It is condescending. It robs a society of the potential value of the smaller markets' contributions to that universal narrative.

Honored Burden admittedly is an interpretation of personal experiences from a little corner of the earth. Its value may or may not extend beyond a certain market. Limited markets' stories need to be told. A book reviewer's retorts can be so weighted in industry norms that outliers are cast as disposables. We live in a world where twisted values, misinformation, conspiracy theories, and right- and left-wing nonsense are selling like ice water in the desert. We can have vastly different opinions on many things, including religion and politics, without casting one another in the fires of hell. It is what makes America the land of the free. Our love for one another as American family members should rule and reside in the Christian spirit that Jesus taught. Could we, for once, dismiss the usual hype of popularity as the standard-bearer for what is valuable or relevant?

Introduction

The American citizenship is arguably the most valuable award in the world. It is an idea for which many have risked life, limb, and family in shabby boats to reach the shores. Others around the globe still dream of getting that one chance at it. For some, it has been a burden, too complicated and too hypocritical to reconcile.

Not always true to its ideas, America is a place of tragedy and triumph. Its citizens have endured—some famous, others infamous. It is those of less notoriety who best represented the strength of those ideas of freedom over the years. Freedom is a remarkable thing with endless intangible dividends. Its cost must never be forgotten. I am proud to promote and carry the banner a little further.

I embrace the humiliation and strength of my parents and my parents' parents to generations unknown. I encourage others to imagine the benefit to which we have inherited and our obligation to continue to push for a more perfect union. Amid all the things that have gone wrong, we are survivors and thrivers—the product of the enormous strength of ideas.

The burden of freedom has been carried around the world with honor, while it was dishonored at home. It is that burden and strength that are embedded in my thoughts and opinions. I seek not to offend, insult, or destroy any person, idea, place, or thing; my apologies to all who interpret my words differently. I explore various topics, narrative, and agendas. It is from this gift of free expression that I can share my life as I have experienced it. I tried to stay humble and honest to my spirit, my calling, and my purpose. I hope I have inspired, encouraged, entertained, and promoted more conversations.

Throughout this book, my thoughts never left those hard-earned sacrifices of yesterday. For those, I am deeply blessed. When I think of what I have gone through, I am instantly humbled by those who have come before me. It is where my strength and expressions get life, and hopefully, live on in you. Freedom and the idea of liberty are what all Americans have been promised. Promises unfulfilled, in all hypocrisy, must not cause us to lose sight of the triumph and magnificence of the ongoing journey. There is respect and responsibility woven in these ideas of freedom that are a part of a checkered and cherished past. Opting for an autocracy because of the checkered dimension of our past would be the ultimate dishonor to the triumphs and an errant look away from the prize. It would do unimaginable and endless harm to the accomplishments of the past, and it would tarnish the pursuit of happiness. Freedom is indeed an honored burden to be embraced and built upon for and by succeeding generations.

Acknowledgments

Thanks to Marilyn Brimmage for her initial project and consultation with the book. Thanks to Jennifer Dupuis for her ideas, technical expertise, and organizational skills and for cleaning up my editorial missteps. Thanks to my partner, Paula Fleming, and the rest of my Family First Support Center family for support, for allowing "me time," and for providing a wealth of ideas and stories for this book.

Chapter 1

Family Ties

Everybody Plays the Fool Sometimes

I have heard many in the older generations talking about teenage silliness as if it is a condition confined to the present era. Although we may have long forgotten, if the truth is known, there are probably some moments of cognitive lapses in our own lives that would bear a scary resemblance to what we see in our teenagers today.

This is not to give any irresponsible behavior a reprieve, but I am going to reveal one that would erupt into some tongue wagging and head shaking regardless of what generation it occurs.

After an evening of work at St. Andrew Presbyterian College (currently St. Andrews University) in Laurinburg, North Carolina, my brother Lenwood; my friends, Curtis and Bobby; my cousin Alphonso; and I all grouped in two automobiles for a ride back home when suddenly, the drivers (my brother Lenwood and my friend Curtis) decided it was Daytona time.

Without a plan and with no purpose or any urging from anyone, they began to drag race. Some immediate thoughts came into my mind after, of course, we were all going to die. These were that this type of racing—with no finish line or checkered flag, no rules or caution flags, and no oversight or red flags—to me, made no sense. It also meant our destination was unknown.

All of a sudden, testosterone took over followed by a burst of egomania, and I found myself caught up in one of two vehicles moving down the road at breakneck speed and so close to each other that I could have reached out and touched the other car. We started going around curves, taking up both sides of the road and blowing through intersections like they had green lights hanging from the stop signs. My first thought was to hit someone or something, and since I did not have access to the brake, I concluded that striking the driver would have meant hitting a ditch or a tree. I finally settled on hitting the floor for a little prayer just because there was no other place left.

What might have been exciting to the drivers or a test of nerves and horsepower went beyond the pale of foolishness in my mind. Although I did not initiate it or encourage it, it was the type of dragnet that anyone could get caught up in, especially teenagers, where daringness runs high and sensibility runs low.

Perhaps some sense and luck kicked in when the last intersection we blew through was just seconds ahead of a crossing vehicle. As I looked back to observe the car passing through, I wondered, as in a game of Russian roulette, how many more empty intersections we had left. It seemed everyone was angling for an advantage or, at least, to get to a point where one could claim a clear victory or where the other one would have to admit defeat. However, with no finish line in sight and the two drivers operating with probably less sense than they started, I resigned myself to the fact that the outcome of this contest was up to God.

When this wild ride and near-fatal experience finally came to an end and the dust and fuss settled, I could not believe each driver was calling themselves the winner by claiming victories on certain stretches of the highway. I thought to myself, *After all this, now I am even more upset if there is not a clear winner because calling this nonsense a draw just meant there was still a score to settle and plenty of road left for round two of this idiocy before someone could be declared the winning fool.*

Famous Cuts

It seemed as if every other Sunday morning came weekly. It was that dreaded haircut day. We did not have a car, horse, or buggy, so our mode of transportation was "Mack and Charlie." Yes, we had to walk. The elder brothers would march the younger ones in single files for two or three miles to our cousin's house for a twenty-five-cent or fifty-cent haircut.

Cousin Floyd was the barber, and no, he was not licensed, certified, or even dignified. Once the cutting began, we never knew what type of cut we would get. He never asked. It was the cut of the day—whatever he decided or felt like giving at the time. Sometimes a bowl was put on the head to cut around. If it were not right, he would make it fit. If it meant a couple of gaps, oh well, maybe he would fix it in two weeks.

Ringworms were common in that era for many of the children in our neighborhood. I did not know if the barber did anything about ringworms, as he moved from head to head. Because our haircuts were cheap, the barber probably cut corners on clipper maintenance. Pricey sanitation practices were not in the budget. Inexpensive haircuts came with risk. Whatever would that be, maybe the barber said a little prayer. Sometimes, cousin Melvin helped his brother Floyd. As an understudy, I was almost sure he was not licensed either. Hop McDougal and, later, Neint Douglas cut our hair. They were all uncertified. The only prior experience barbers had at the time would have been clipping or shaving farm animals, unless they practiced on their sister's dolls.

The walk to our cousin's house was a grueling one, and the youngest male led the pack. The "rules of the road" speech came from my brother Gary Jr. or my brother James before we departed as if I did not know how to stay out of the way of one or two vehicles that would pass us on the road to and from the barber's house. Everyone had sizeable families back then, so we could not count on getting a ride to or from the barbershop. We would get that "rules of the road" speech again before we would walk back home. We marched like soldiers. I would have made a good soldier. When we got too far out

13

of line, a smack on the side of the head was a reminder to get in line. It indicated which way I needed to move, back or forth. All confusions were straightened out with a harder smack. Marchers were not allowed to talk in the line to and from the barbershop. Once at the barbershop, you had to sit down and wait your turn to be tortured. Instructions were to sit down, be still, and wait. The cutting would begin almost instantly, with no questions or suggestions on the type of haircut.

Initially, scissors were the tools of choice. Then came the manual clippers that required more oil than the average car. The barber's hands were greasier than Mom's biscuits. Later there were electric clippers with no size guards. Cousin Floyd would just do his best to gauge what needed to be taken off. The barber never explained cuts, such as high and tight, close fade, or a little off the top. There were no pictures on the wall as examples of haircuts. Cousin Floyd cut our hair like he was always in a hurry. It was like he was late for something. It was not until years later we learned he had to get to morning service or deal with his mother, Aunt Maggie Bell.

What made these cuts famous were the lasting memories or impressions I received from this dreadful two-mile ordeal to and from the crude reception in the chair. My daddy made it mandatory that we keep to the two-week schedule, rain or snow, so that we could keep our "snap sack" cleaned up. Well, cousin Floyd perhaps did his best. His lack of certification was not his fault. Maybe the old and dilapidated equipment were responsible for the painful and memorable ordeal, not his skill level. Either way, the haircuts would always be famous.

Horne Section

It is not a new phenomenon that kids become bored in school and wander off on nonacademic activities that tend to disrupt the class. It is also not unique or unusual that peer influence often plays a part. The following are two incidents that occurred in Mr. Horne's class: one of which I was a part of, and the other is where I was the butt of the joke. Since Mr. Horne was my twelfth-grade teacher, it confirms that peer influence and silliness exist throughout high school.

The first incident occurred while the teacher was out of the class. One of my classmates came up with a brilliant idea that we would turn our desks backward so when Mr. Horne returned to the room, he would be looking at the back of our heads. Solidarity would force him to come to the rear to teach. I knew the idea was stupid and that I was being challenged as a punk if I did not go along. I knew better, and in the face of common sense, I succumbed to the foolishness to appease my classmates. Mr. Horne often presented a quiet and controlled demeanor. We were just trying to get a rise. When he did return to class, Mr. Horne hit the roof. He paused, took a deep breath, and told us we had exactly three seconds to get our desks turned around. Then he started counting. Three seconds did not give a person much time to look around and see what everyone else was doing. I heard desks moving. I guess that meant solidarity broke. I figured we had a good run, but the game was over. For our joke, we got an extra homework assignment.

Many of my classmates were jokesters. I must admit I was also a little mischievous. The second incident occurred when I was out of the class. The classroom location allowed students to see a person approaching across the yard. I was walking toward class, and some classmates were monitoring my movement in the yard. They hid behind the door, and when I entered, I got mugged supposedly by deranged, out-of-control fans shouting "James Brown!" because my hair resembled the style of the R & B singer/performer. The day before, I had my sisters Mary and Linda work long and hard on my hair to help give me that look. It was not easy or free, yet it took my classmates seconds to dismantle. My hair was standing all over my head. It had been straightened with a hot iron. There was not much I could do to get it to return to form. My classmates were explaining they did not know what came over them at the sighting of James Brown; they could not help themselves. I knew that was a bunch of crap. It was old-school player hating. When I finally got up from under the weight of bodies, I was unable to tell whose idea it was or who did what. I shook it off, gathered myself, and headed to the bathroom. The "Don King" look was not in yet, but I needed to do something with my hair because it was a distraction, even to me. I looked a mess. I thought about going home. However, telling my father I would be missing school because of a little embarrassment would not have gone over very well. I settled on watering my hair down to shrink it to a manageable length so I could form a different style. I became the hardest-working man on my hair for about ten minutes. It made me tardy for the class for which I received a consequence. My classmates had already gotten their laughs, so I could have looked like Lena Horne when I returned, they would not care. Lena Horne's maiden name was Calhoun, so a celebrity mugging on her account would have made more sense.

My classmates' so-called sudden brush with fame was the kind of foolishness that teenagers manufacture. Striking back at them would have gotten me in more trouble. Besides, it was the same type of silliness I probably spearheaded a couple of times in the past. I am glad they got a good laugh. I hope everyone who joined in the foolishness at least thought the hairdo they messed up was a good resemblance to James Brown's or at least knew who he was.

King of the Bench

During my elementary years at R.B. Dean School, kids would gather around an area on the playground where there was an old bench, probably a relic from a baseball field where the players sat. Anyone feeling tough or lucky could attempt to walk from one end to the other while dismissing all challengers whose goals were to either disrupt that goal or complete his goal of reaching the opposite side of where he started. Once an opponent was wrestled or thrown from the bench, others would rise and take his place. To be crowned "king of the bench," one had to be willing to take on all comers, friends, enemies, classmates, underclassmen, and upperclassmen. The cry was always, "Show no mercy!" So if little brother got in the way, he had to be dealt with in the same harsh manner as anyone else. Those were the rules of the bench, although I did not think anyone ever saw them written anywhere. One had to be swift, strong, nimble, slippery, agile, and sometimes lucky to make it through to the other side.

It was a game or exercise in strategy that many of the students participated in before school started. It also meant that some students reported to homeroom class late, dirty, and sometimes with their clothes torn or ripped from tussling. I could remember schoolmates and classmates scrambling, trying to make quick use of the restroom areas to clean themselves up as best as they could in preparation for class. Everyone knew that even if one had been fortunate enough to be crowned king of the bench, when that king entered the classroom, there was only one king or queen, as the case may be, and that was the teacher. It was not fashionable or tolerated to report to class with a shirttail out or shirts unbuttoned even if some other student arranged it that way.

Many took the challenge, including myself, and many failed, including me. But that did not stop us from trying again and again. It was supposed to be good clean fun and an early test of manhood. However, there were some accused of using unfair and underhanded tactics, in the form of tripping, that would anger an opponent to the point of wanting to "take it to the street"—I mean, take it beyond the bench.

Of all the "king of the bench" battles I witnessed, the one that still stood out in my mind as most memorable ended in a draw. It involved two of my friends, Frankie and Carnell. Although Carnell was an underclassman to Frankie, their match that started on the bench seemed legendary because it lasted for so long it appeared to be a stalemate. But somehow the game that began quickly and long endured ended with a takedown to the bench. It continued to the ground after falling from the bench. It was turning into a street brawl and a test of wills that culminated in leaving both opponents leaning on each other and exhausted. I thought to myself, *With all the hugging they are doing, they may as well kiss and say goodbye.* There finally was a ceasefire. They walked away from each other as if they had enough, without a declaration from either on who was the winner or, in their case, who was the king of the bench and the king of the grounds around it.

17

Let There Be Light

In my early childhood, the light was a luxury we did not have. I am talking about electric lights for illuminating the dark or providing heat. We had no electricity, so homework was planned strategically. I had to make the best use of solar energy before it was fashionable. It was challenging during the winter months because sometimes after an-hour-and-a-half ride on the school bus to get home, it was either near dark or already dark, and you know the hogs and chickens had to get fed before I could eat or do any homework.

In my house, it was always "first thing is first." Chores were first, but even if darkness caught me, it meant I had to do it in the dark. There was no such thing as too dark to cut or gather firewood. These things had to be taken care of before such trivialities as eating.

Sorry, I neglected to mention that I had to get out of my school clothes almost as soon as I got in the house. I maybe had three outfits for the week. Being the youngest son meant I took everyone's hand-me-downs. I was the third youngest of eleven. By the time the clothes got to me—the constant battering from the washboards, the continuous abuse with lye soap, and the rough treatment from my elder brothers—I could be assured the clothing had a different color and texture and all identifying tags were long gone. I did not know what I was wearing; it could have been my sisters' clothes.

Younger members of the family had the protection of the elder siblings. That is how it was supposed to work. They were required to take care of the younger ones, whether they wanted to or not. I am pretty sure as I mention this, some of the elder siblings in today's families are gesturing that my little sister(s) and brother(s) are not my children and my parents cannot make me take care of them unless they pay me. Oh, how far we have come or strayed because my elder siblings did not have that option and did expect to continue sticking their feet under my parents' table.

With elder siblings' protection came their authority. I had many bosses in the house. I protested a couple of times, but once I found out Daddy signed off on it, there was nothing I could do. It was always better to be knocked down by them than by my father. It was the order of things, so I settled in and did as I was told. Let me get back to the light.

When it came to my schoolwork, I was pretty engaged on what was going on in the classroom; so when it came to doing homework as darkness fell, it became a little tricky to find enough light to complete assignments. I could never say something like, "I am going to be using the kerosene lamp to do my homework." First, I had better not put my hands on either one of the two lamps we had. I was not old enough to be trusted to move the lamp from one area of the house to another without possibly burning the house down. I was not sure why my eldest brother, Gary Jr., did not have the same restriction. He would stumble and fall over a flat floor. The houses we lived in back then were composed of so much dry wood that they were capable of catching fire by the heat from the wood-burning stove. With the amount of kerosene spilled on the floor over the years, a dropped lamp would probably blow up the house. It was not our house, so we would have been so indebted to the sharecropper owner that our grandchildren would still be working off the debt.

Wherever the light went, I had to follow so I could complete my homework. You would think my elder siblings would see my trying to do my homework and keep the light in one place and be generous enough to ask me how they could facilitate me finishing my homework. I could not remember it ever happening. I could remember moving often. If my sister Naomi had the light, she probably hit me in the head just for looking at the lamp like I wanted to say something.

Turning the lamp out at night was decided by elder siblings with little or no regard for the younger ones. Task completion, when an elder sibling had other ideas, was an exercise in futility. It taught me how to adjust, adapt, and become one with my environment. I grew so conscientious of my situation that I became master of my universe. I honed adaptability skills that were transferable to the classroom and later in life. Having a lot of bosses made me good at following directions. Even today, I am good at doing as told. I got lots of practice. You could say I saw the light early. Years of following the light lit up my life.

My, My, My (Aunt Myonia)

Born in 1920, she was a spitfire, had a sharp tongue, and was blunt. Some thought she was mean and rude. My niece Chimere certainly got an unforgettable taste of her when she begged to accompany her father and three uncles on a trip to Philadelphia. That was Aunt My, the baby sister of my father and the one accused of going rouge long before Sarah Palin was born. I did not know her in her younger life when she traveled the world singing gospel with the likes of James Cleveland, the Gospel All-Stars, and others. Aunt My spoke about that part of her life with admiration and shame. She had partaken in all-night drinking and partying. She said she faked the alcohol and some of the laughter to be accepted. To her family, she forsook all she was taught and was disgraceful. She said she stayed away from some family gatherings because of open ridicule by almost everyone. She continued to live her life as she declared it did not hurt anyone, and she did not believe she was disgracing the family.

She said her father died when she was four or five. She barely remembered him. She recalled being at the head of his bed before his funeral, hearing him call her Lillie, one of her elder sisters' names. "He didn't even know my name," she said, and then he was gone. My aunt told me her mother died when she was a teenager. It gave her an opportunity to get out of the south. She could not wait to leave the Jim Crow farm and went the first chance she got. She referred to sharecropping as a legal robbery because that is what she believed the landowners did to all the black farmers. They knew they could do it without worrying about being punished.

She moved to live with her sister in Washington, DC, and later to Philadelphia to stay with her eldest brother. Her sister Lillie and brother John C., who were instrumental in helping her out of the south, were viewed with mixed emotions. On the one hand, she was grateful; on the other, she was disappointed. Instead of the landowners taking her money, it was her family. The upbringing in her generation meant, as the baby, she had little or no say-so when conversing with siblings. She did grow to challenge her elder sister Lillie from time to time.

She described her elder brother John C. as being like a father. Not once did she ever disobey or back talk. The constant treatment as a child forced her to determine it was best to seek independence elsewhere. That was when the rumors started swirling that she was loose and wild. These rumors persisted for the remainder of her life. No matter how hard she tried to atone for her youthful indiscretion, she was unable to shake it.

She said she did not find love twice, even though she was married twice. She refused to call her first marriage love. She said there were no words sorry enough to describe her first husband. She described her second husband as the exact opposite—loving, thoughtful, and kind. She also experienced motherhood twice but did not have much of a relationship with either child.

She was very devoted to her extended family. She attended her siblings' and their spouses' funerals throughout the years. I saw her on these occasions dressed in those furs and mink coats and always thought she was classy and glamorous. She was an occasional sighting in my early childhood. I asked who she was and where she fit in the family order. As my parents' siblings dwindled, it became apparent to me where she belonged in the birth order. Some of my aunts and cousins were not that far apart in age, so there were times when I referred to some of my cousins as aunts or uncles and vice versa.

Once, I attempted to quiet Aunt My in my office by reminding her that it was a place of business and that she needed to lower her voice. She told this CEO, "Who are you talking to, boy? I ain't loud, but I will show you what loud is when I come over there and crawl all over you." I left her in my office and went down the hall. I figured she would burn out faster than I could put her out.

In later years, she surfaced more and was the only one of her family members standing by the turn of the century. She spent her last years with me in a lot at family reunions I hosted. She lived with me for the last six months of her life. Over the years, she certainly did not lose her fire. She had plenty left for her nieces and nephews, including me.

I never lost my love and fondness for her. My aunt's sharp tongue continued to cause some—as in the early years—to misunderstand her and never fully appreciate her wisdom, big heart, and love of family.

Rooftop

In a conversation with a childhood friend, I remembered an incident I had long forgotten. It was a routine activity during my early childhood.

I am not sure which one of my brothers took the plunge; although I think it was Gerone. He is the primary character in what I am about to describe. I am reasonably sure it was not me.

When we finally got a television, I believe I was about eleven or twelve years old. The first reception was from rabbit-ear antennas that required certain sophistication in the application of aluminum foil or a clothes hanger at the end of the rabbit ears extensively to access a greater range in reception.

Perhaps a year after getting our first television, I think we moved up to an outside antenna that was on the rooftop. Well, our extension in reception range did not come without its drawbacks or, shall I say, hazards. I could recall one or two occasions when our rooftop antenna needed some adjustment. It meant someone must climb to the top of the roof and turn the antenna. It was usually located somewhere near the chimney. When one reached the top of the roof, a little yelling along with excellent listening ears is required—at least enough to recognize the sound to stop or halt. If the antenna was turned slightly beyond where it should be, the yelling from inside drowned out instructions needed for proper adjustment up top.

On this day, the A-frame tin roof was a little wet and tricky. During all the yelling and screaming to adjust the antenna, suddenly it turned into a noise like timber or SOS. Faster than one could say "Oops," our antenna adjuster was seen through the window, coming in hot and adjusting airspeed in preparation for a hard landing. I recalled seconds before the crash-landing, there were rapid footsteps on the tin roof, and then suddenly there was silence. I knew the steps were too fast to catch the ladder. It was discarded like a tool in the way of progress.

This incident highlighted the dangers of flight without a license or parachute, especially by inexperienced television watchers. We weighed all future program receptions and adjustments against the likelihood of another rooftop mishap. The reward of a better reception of the TV show *The Lone Ranger* or *Lassie* always outweighed the consequences.

Submerged Nuggets

Recently, something conjured up some hidden nuggets in my childhood that I had long pushed down because of the pain and shame associated with them.

As the son of a sharecropper, I could remember my father talking about settling with the landowner or negotiating to use a small share of the property as a garden just for his family. It was difficult tending the landowner's farm in its entirety and providing for his children as practically free servants to the landowner's beck and call.

Each year, as he settled after working extremely hard himself with his children, somehow the only profit went to the owner. The owner moved up, but my father would find himself in the hole. The owner would buy a new car almost every year. My father barely afforded to keep food on the table. He borrowed money from the owner just to get started for a new year. It would leave him in a deeper hole than the one for which he started.

I think my father found it was harsh and painful to admit defeat to a reputable foe. No matter how hard he tried, failure was always standing before him saying, "That's all you got!" Everything in him was telling him, "You may as well give up," "You cannot win," "Too much is stacked against you, and "Why don't you make it easy for yourself and surrender?" My father admitted that there were times when defeat got the better of him. Even if he felt he was out of options, "no" was not in him. He could not bring himself to say these three words: I give up. Instead, he would say, "I am going one more year, and I know I said that last year and the year before. But I am just not ready to throw in the towel." So he kept getting up year after year until defeat finally came to him and said, "Let's call a truce." My father wanted no part of that, so he told defeat, "After all these years of battling with you, you want me to call it even. When it comes to settling, I won't settle for anything but up."

He would accept anything but total surrender from defeat, even though his hands were weak. He was hanging on to his last son (me), who wanted no parts of the farm. His health had begun to decline, but his voice against defeat was as loud as ever. He would say, "I want to say, 'Let me buy a car, boss man, and you go into next year borrowing from me.' I want to hear defeat howl for once even as my hearing fades." I carried my father's final words as if they were the same as Coach Vince Lombardi's: "I haven't ever lost a game; time ran out."

As his last son and the one who wanted nothing to do with the farm, his relationship with defeat had been passed on to me. I, like my father, am against making peace with defeat. Those hidden nuggets of pain and shame rest and reside deep inside me. Every time "quit" and "give up" show their faces, it calls up my father's pains and shame of the constant yearly battles with defeat. In a sharecropper's world, constant failure attempted to rob him of his dignity and stood in the way of him providing for his family.

In my book, *In the Shadow of Sacrifice*, there are many stories. My father's epic battles with defeat continue in me as one of those stories. I am an eternal enemy of failure. Defeat, I know not, and my encouragement to everyone is to get to know the winner in you. Do not take up time and counsel with failure. When defeat tries to partner with you, run far and fast. It is a ploy for more time to work its fangs in you. Though my story as a stutterer is also one of poverty, hunger, illiteracy, abuse, and pain, it is one of the humble beginnings with defeat as a constant companion or nuisance, depending on how you choose to take up company. Your conversations with failure should be of continual rejection. Let defeat know that God created you to be undefeatable.

Chapter 2

Education

A Teacher's Teacher

I remembered all my teachers and was always fond of them. However, as I thought about my time in the tenth grade, I could not believe the many funny or light moments in the classroom when suddenly it would dawn on me. Mrs. Brayboy, my tenth-grade teacher, did not allow any light moments. I was afraid to move a muscle in her class. When I discussed her with my classmates, we all felt the same way. No one in my circle laughed and played with her. She was all business. Since she was extremely hard to read, I decided I needed to keep my rude little remarks to myself.

Learning was first in her class, and I did excel. It was not that education was unimportant in other teachers' courses, but when the mission (at least in my mind) was unwavering, you stayed clued in. And that was what I did.

Now that I have been a teacher and have worked in the classroom, I understand clearer what Mrs. Brayboy was trying to accomplish. I also guess my perception of her was tremendously flawed and influenced by immature peers.

She gave everyone what they needed. I am sure some of them required more no-nonsense discipline than me. She is the real embodiment of what a teacher should be if a student is to become what he or she should be. Knowing one's students is not permitting their immature, negative selves to ground and define them. Therefore, I had to drop the mischievousness that I was accustomed to because it subtracted from my learning. Not being able to recall funny moments in class is not a bad thing, especially when I can remember learning a lot. She cared enough about her students to not allow them to get away with underperformance. Thanks, Mrs. Brayboy. We could use more of you today as a teacher's teacher.

Do You Have a Better Plan?

As a school counselor at Dillard Middle School in Goldsboro, North Carolina, I was challenged many times by students uttering the expression that school was a waste of time and they were not learning anything, so why wouldn't they quit?

Initially, I would listen, as counselors are trained to do, and would let them talk themselves out, maybe just long enough for them to hear how ridiculous they sounded. Of course, I could come up with lots of information and statistics about the average lifetime income of high school graduates versus dropouts. I would share the alarming number of dropouts who end up in prison or shot or mangled from a career in crime. I would explain how college graduates earn more options for life's opportunities. I would never pass my students' comments off as unworthy or not worth discussing, but when I kept hearing the same remarks by more than a few students, I began to wonder if there was a training school I was unaware of that was teaching this nonsense. Some students would come armed with research to counter my research. I would always get the one about Bill Gates dropping out of college. I also heard that LeBron James never went beyond high school and that most of their heroes, such as Jay-Z, Lil Wayne, and Mary J. Blige, dropped out of high school. One student went old school on me and said neither Tina Turner nor James Brown graduated high school; even Elvis Presley did not go to college.

I think they kept bringing me counter information because the word got out that I had little patience for nonsense. I was always in a hurry to get them back to class, even if it was PE.

Students told me teachers and counselors, for that matter, did not make the kind of money they intended to make, so why should they stay in school for that little change? The students would say, "Now the rappers and ballplayers—that's money and the kind of which we will be making." Sometimes, they would say, "Now if you think we should stay in school to be a rapper, singer, or professional ballplayer, then we are all ears."

I would say, "Okay, since you gave me a way out, let us talk about those careers as rappers, singers, or professional ballplayers. Present me the evidence that you have thought this out and have been working on a plan, a business plan if you will, about how you intend to get all this big money being a rapper, singer, or ballplayer. How have you been preparing yourself? When Bill Gates dropped out of college, he got into something that had been a part of a plan for a few years. If middle school is in the way of keeping you from achieving things you can't wait to obtain, then provide me the well-thought-out plan on how you will get from where you are today to where you intend to be by the same time it will take you to complete high school." I would say, "In fact, there is nothing that keeps you from pursuing that big money goal now while you are attending school. Young people have the energy to do more than one thing at a time."

Some students even told me that they were going to make it on *American Idol*. At the time of this writing, *American Idol* has had over four million auditions in its twelve seasons with only twelve winners. US Park Ranger Roy C. Sullivan holds the world record for the number of times being struck by lightning: seven. Students thinking about dropping out of school without a plan yet expecting to win on *American Idol* have a better chance of breaking Mr. Sullivan's record.

Let me share this conversation with all students contemplating on dropping out of school: Until you come up with a better plan, continue working the school plan as if it is the only plan you got because it is.

Chapter 3

─◆─

Living and Loving Life

Child II Adult

Childhood is but for one reason: preparation for adulthood. In the American culture, adulthood is somewhere between the ages of eighteen and twenty-one. In some other countries, it is much less—around thirteen or fourteen.

To keep things nice and neat and to help those who are not good at math, follow my scenario. I am going to stick with the American culture and use age twenty as my example. Let us say the average life expectancy is eighty years. A person has one-fourth of a life to prepare for the final three-fourths. Once a person reaches adulthood, prepared or not, that person cannot go back to childhood. If that person is unprepared to navigate the challenges of adulthood, immeasurable disruptive and destructive childhood behaviors will follow into adulthood.

So who is responsible for preparing a child for adulthood? Before you give me the obvious answer, let me provide some more information. If I bring a pencil in a room, who is responsible for it? Who will it affect if I do not take responsibility for it? Likely, it will have little or no effect on anyone. If I bring a bomb in a room, who is responsible for it? Who will it affect if I do not take responsibility for it? If I leave the bomb, can you just ignore it as you did the pencil? If people bring children in this world and do not treat them as seri-

28

ously as we would a bomb and do not prepare them for adulthood, it affects us all, and more than the parent must take responsibility.

If we look out our windows and see a devastating fire in another town, then pull our shades down as if it doesn't concern us, can we expect the person in the next city to come to our aid when the fire is burning at our door? That is where we are today. Our house is on fire. The sprinkler is activated. It is a little water here and there, and it is not amazingly effective. It is too late for a casual intervention. To treat a child like we would the pencil will have a devastating effect on all of us.

Beyond the parents, we have three significant institutions, along with a catchall category, responsible for helping to prepare children for adulthood:

1. the family—which includes a nucleus and extensions of roles, including siblings, grandparents, guardians, uncles, aunts, stepparents, cousins, and other relatives
2. the schools—teachers, administrators, counselors, etc.
3. the religious institutions—churches, mosques, synagogues, and other places of worship
4. the community at-large

Two words have entered our institutions—disruption and corruption. Let me speak about some of the institutional solutions and some of the challenges we are experiencing with these. Let me start with the family. Preparation of the child for adulthood should begin in the womb well before the child is born. Using tobacco, alcohol, drugs, and other toxins is poor preparation. Some are responsible for preparing a child for adulthood while preparing for adulthood themselves. It is obvious they do not qualify for something for which they have yet to finish. It is a ten-alarm fire. All available units are required for the preparation of our children for adulthood. Disruption of the processes and the corruption of personnel must be managed better by everyone. Disaster is imminent without all hands on deck and maximum support from all areas and institutions of care. It is a #MeToo moment.

Fate

Being a living witness of what amounts to a wholesale failure in love, finance, and overall development, one must wonder how much of that is fate or how much is design. If we look at life as an endeavor with a history of measurable generational outcomes, when these results are consistently counter to the expectations and hard work of law-abiding citizens, why wouldn't there be a pause to examine or investigate the causes of so much failure? No business could long endure if it tolerated such a dismal record over an extended period without calling for a task committee to review and address the cause and effect. So why aren't we up and armed and on full alert about the rate of failures in life? Sure, there are some successes, but the vast majority of people, by their accounts, agree they have failed to accomplish what they set out to do in life. Is this fate, or is there a systemic set of rules and operations in play that creates these outcomes?

Now we know faith without work is dead, so I am not talking about those unfamiliar with work. The lazy who are among the failure get what they deserve. I am referring to those who do nothing but work and cannot lift themselves beyond paycheck to paycheck. Who is to blame? Isn't this the land of opportunities?

Some segments of the population are faring better than others—that 1 percent the media always seems to say is getting more prosperous. What is behind that tiny part of the people that appears to be rising and aspiring, while an extensive portion appears to be in free fall?

I believe my father worked long and hard for many years. He ended up broke, destitute, and dejected about his situation before his death. How it is that one is born in the land of opportunity, live and grow freely around and among these opportunities for seventy years or more, yet somehow accidentally end up with less than one started? And this occurs on a regular basis.

Is it a card trick played on the masses? The masses seem to be enjoying and accepting it as the way it is. There's no sense in fretting about it. Have the masses given up on trying to figure out how to move beyond failure? Maybe they have lost track of the score and think they are winning. Is it that the masses know something is wrong but cannot figure it out and just figure there is nothing they can do about it? Are all these failures accidents or just a run of bad luck? What is wrong with the script if it is only working brilliantly for a few? Is it working just as designed? Are there rewards for failures that garnish opportunities and lessons that are greater than the sum of all failures?

When there are likely failures at a higher percentage in one segment of the population than another and the one doing the predicting is receiving the favor, something is amiss. We must examine the indicators of failure for structural issues or simply put a fix. We must account for poor individual choices and missed opportunities. It is highly unlikely that one can go from birth to death without encountering opportunities. Is systemic unpreparedness a design or happenstance? Are preset rigged structures a part of that design? Study the design and figure out how to not be a part of the formula. Fate, at some level, is a part of a script. Each of society's scenarios is different. Some cultures do not permit much movement beyond the script. Even in a free society—with individual choices, legal remedies, and protections—the pitfalls are there. It all comes down to more than just being different. Different must be a part of a well-thought-out plan with backup plans designed to increase the percentage of success and limit the degree of failure.

Following the script in making mortgage payments will amount to a successful conclusion for the bank. That design is not the most successful for the borrower. Devising and following a plan that takes more off the principal balance would be a better script for the borrower.

It is what happens in life. Not being aware of design flaws slanted against the individual account for moving around as if there are no hazards. Most walk in that manner, unaware that it defaults to the script. It all but guarantees a predictable high failure rate. Some call it fate. I call it fate with deficiencies.

Good for You

Humans are marketable commodities. Which do you prefer— the celery stick or the peppermint stick? Which is good for us, and which is good to us—the GNC store or the ABC store? One promotes living well, the other pushes feeling well. One is good for us, and the other is good to us. Which one do you prefer?

Marketers are excellent at appealing to our appetite and feelings over and above what we know is right. If we are not concerned about whether it is good for us, why should someone interested in maximizing profit be concerned? Marketers are looking out for their best interests. What? You want them to look out for yours too? We expect others to do the thing that is good for us when we do not do it for ourselves and are disappointed when they do not. A diabetic expects a doctor to prescribe something that will ameliorate all poor eating habits while relieving the diabetic of any nutritional changes or responsibility.

What are we supposed to be doing with our time while others are doing for us what we should be doing for ourselves? What are we going to do about not doing what is right for us? By doing what is best for us, we do what is best to us.

If You Are Rich or Poor

In this article, I will pose and leave many open questions to ponder. For the sake of simplicity, I am going to use *richness* and *wealth* interchangeably although I realize they have slightly different meanings. If you are rich, who or what threatens your abundance? If you are broke, who and what threaten your poverty? A favorite argument for the rich is the elimination of entitlement programs. A case for the poor is opposition to the removal or curtailment of poverty programs. Are the rich less wealthy because of these programs? Are the poor more prosperous because of these programs? Have we reached a tipping point where the poor have got enough, far beyond basic survival and human needs? Is now the time to cut them off because it is putting the rich in jeopardy of being poor? There are arguments to whether poverty programs are helping or hurting the poor. Are the rich in better situations because they have made more sacrifices and better decisions than the poor? If so, why should they be mandated to subsidize poor folks? Should those, through virtually no effort of their own, who inherited or fell into wealth be less responsible for sharing the wealth? Had the giver meant it for someone else, they would have given it to them when they were alive. The problem, according to the rich, is, they are being forced against their freedom. Is it true the rich took advantage of the opportunities to become rich and the poor failed to make benefits of those same opportunities? Is it merely a choice to be poor or be wealthy? Why should the poor have everything the rich have when they have sat on their butts while the rich worked their butt off? Is it fair to the rich or anyone who has busted their butts to get where they are not to give up part of their fortune to someone less fortunate maybe due to laziness? These are points to ponder, and I agree with many of them, with some clarifications.

Because all poverty looks the same, how do we separate the working poor—those who contribute significantly to the productivity of wealth—from the lazy poor? Are the working poor not much different because they have been lazy and poor at making decisions with their money, therefore, deserve the same condition, or were they slighted by a system set up by the rich that reimbursed them inadequately for their productivity?

Poverty and wealth are murky in America and many other countries for that matter. It is so complicated that it stretches back to the richness of the birth of the nation and beyond. An unbalanced understanding of the past's contribution to the present undermines one's credibility when commenting about the evolution of wealth.

Disagreement is expected on the reasons for the disparity between the rich and poor. Not everyone will acknowledge or appreciate the other's position. Some rich says they already know, end of discussion. The poor believes the system is not for them. For many, their choice comes down to settling for a lifetime of poverty and getting what is available within that position. Neither wish to know the plight of the other, at least not to the degree it diminishes their position. If the poor believes the rich's wealth came off the backs of the poor, then redistribution is the only fair thing. This is perhaps true in some cases, but the shoe would not fit everyone. Unjust penalization of the rich is as inequitable as forcing all poor to give up all noncon-

tributory entitlement programs. To be fair, plenty rich people volun-
tarily give to the poor, and there is a great deal of poor who do not
want anything from the rich. They are just as firm against individuals
being forced or obligated to do for them against their will.

The central point is, how do we make the most of what is available? How can resources created by more than the rich best be dis-
tributed to indeed add value to the life and condition of the poor,
the middle class, and the rich? There is room for a common ground's
argument.

Poverty is more complicated than the absence of riches. From the
beginning of the American experience, when wealth was being created,
poverty was also being built by the same forces. Opportunities to own
slaves, land, properties, and ideas were pathways to riches. Opportunities
to be a slave, to work the land, to property, and to not share the profits
of labor established poverty. Profits can be reinvested by the rich to create more profit. The poor's money ran out before the month, so there
was nothing left to reinvest. The rich may say the poor did not share in
the risk, and the poor will counter that the threat for them was far more
significant than any peril the rich could ever imagine.

Although the physical barriers to riches were damaging, in my
opinion, the worst of these obstacles was not having opportunities to
the best education and knowledge. It sabotaged the mind in a way
that made it a nonfactor in the alleviation of poverty even once many
of the physical barriers were lessened or removed. By mass-producing
generational populations of poor thinkers within a system of status
quo enablers, it concealed the way out. It masked potentials and led
to an underclass of living, better known as poverty.

To request the rich to assume some accountability for poverty
is to ask them to envision a concept foreign to their way of thinking.
They had access to the best schools. Outcomes associated with lower
levels of thinking is counter to their analytical teaching. There is a
difference between the way the rich and poor figure out things. Both
have produced successful outcomes to their way of thinking. Results
are generational and measurable for both groups.

Absence of the best education and best information is the worst
component of the creation of poverty for the poor. Access to the best

schools is the best component to the creation of wealth for the rich. Not only was the rich able to proceed without any physical barriers but their efforts were also facilitated, encouraged, and expedited by favorable legal and governmental rules and policies. This was the same systems and institutions that erected the barriers that produced learned helplessness in the poor. To top this off, if somehow the poor managed to elude all the systemic barriers and was lucky enough to squeeze education from some unidentified source, its use was forbidden in law. It is these earliest educational barriers that created mental barriers so profound and everlasting that communities are still reeling from the devastation today. Even those who are not beneficiaries of old money or generational wealth and are newcomers to wealth will have to acknowledge—it was their mental faculties that are most responsible for their riches even if they are products of the poverty class. When mental power is eviscerated, there will be a few who will break through. The majority will follow the masses. If one class of people's information and knowledge is deficient and another group is the exemplary, outcomes will be proportionate. Each segment will proceed, unaware of the different origins. In time, both will accept certain norms and promote a narrative that says, "That's the way it is." Both groups will be conscious of a general knowledge of contributions from perhaps two or three generations. As it is with most things, the same is true with poverty and wealth. The devil is in the details. Because many pertinent issues crowd individuals' and families' situations and demand much of one's daily time throughout a lifetime, delving into the details of the origins of poverty and wealth stemming back over ten or eleven generations may be too much to ask even from a most enlightened person. It is this entangled trail of details that form the divide and bridge to the establishment of America's wealth and poverty.

Lost

Father would say, "No matter how hard I work, I seem to get nowhere, lost." Why is this just as true today as it was during his day? Aren't we the species who can take information from one generation, study it, and use it to improve the succeeding generations? What is it that we keep missing that keeps us falling prey to the same mistakes generation after generation?

Many things affect personal achievement. Some things such as politics, religion, race, and gender are beyond our control. To concentrate on those things would be unwise. Unfortunately, it is where many spend a great deal of time. It usually results in complaints and excuses.

The word that I think resonated with my father's situation that is most relevant today to his grandchildren is *preparation*. Lack of preparation continues to emerge as a generational barrier to accomplishment. That one word is a key for all generations. Success happens when preparation and opportunity meet. Hall of Fame coach Jimmy Johnson said it, but he indeed was not the first. We are missing opportunities to advance ourselves because we are unprepared. Preparation is the acquisition of necessary skills and the engineering of enough relevant factors that amount to a controlled maneuver of oneself into a situation where opportunities are likely to arise. Rapper and artist Eminem explained *opportunity* as one shot to seize the moment, to lose yourself, and to never let it go. There is nothing original or extraordinary about the correlation between opportunity and preparedness and their relationship to success; why the aversion to it?

The first requirement to becoming prepared is admitting you are unprepared. Then assess your level of preparedness. Devise a plan to become prepared. Implement the program. Review and evaluate the project for effectiveness. Modify or adjust as needed.

To seize opportunities, you must take ownership of preparation. Benjamin Franklin, John Wooden, and Mark Spitz all said if we fail to prepare, we have prepared to fail. That is the natural consequences of inaction. How many more people need to say it?

In Zig Ziglar's classic *See You at the Top*, he indicated there was more room at the top because few will prepare or do what is required to get there.

Throw down the gauntlet. Start preparation where you are. If you have an eye for an opportunity but are unprepared, opportunities that meet your eye will pass. Relying on stumbling into an opportunity as a strategy is ill-advised, but expecting to take advantage of that opportunity with more stumbling is just foolish.

It has been many years since my father uttered those words about working hard yet feeling lost. Now my father's offspring are in a land with considerably more opportunities. They have had the benefit of three and four generations of history. To be less prepared than a generation that was legally restricted from preparation begs an explanation from all the ancient scholars. To continue to embrace unpreparedness is to put oneself in the same predicament as the denied preparedness of my father's era. For Dad, it was opportunity denied; for his grandchildren, it is an opportunity they let slide. Not being prepared to take advantage of an opportunity produces the same results as not being allowed to take advantage of an opportunity. Father was lost in a barren field. Generations later, his grandchildren are lost in a gold mine.

Message

A message can be a single word or several words that can have many different definitions. I will allow the reader to just think about what that may mean. For this article, I will speak of it in subtle and hidden terms.

When a person speaks about something, he is probably trying to relay a message. A teacher working to drive a point home on a subject is conveying a message. Some words are simple and easily understood. But how about messages shrouded in codes, not quite ready for quick consumption? Their very design is incomplete and represents talking or guiding points to be pondered.

Sometimes when I think of the power of submerged and hidden messages, I think of those, perhaps historically, that determined decisions and outcomes yet were without any author.

What are the messages to kids or the younger generation about bling and the outward display of jewelry when adults, leaders, stars, or unsuspected role models present themselves awash in such ornaments?

Are messages more essential or less relevant today? Are messages specifically and strategically designed to convey and arouse imagination more critical than eyewitness accounts?

Lastly, because of the rudimentary mode of transportation of the era, Jesus, in his lifetime, probably never traveled more than forty or fifty miles from his birthplace. Today, his message resonates throughout nearly the entire globe. That is the power of message.

Misplaced Values

Sound decisions are difficult to come by for many. Emotions and impulses run high when stress levels are unstable. Access to productive counsel is mostly missing among the most immediate circle of friends and family members. We cannot blame people for using what is available. Often they would have done better without the information. Now that Facebook, Instagram, and other Internet and media services are playing a more significant role in decisions, the reliability metrics are much more difficult to manage. In some cases, Mom and Dad are having their challenges or are missing altogether. Grandma and Grandpa may be still getting their groove on and not have time to offer any guidance. They may be just as unreliable. When we throw in the country's love affair with all types of alcohol and drugs, crashing and burning seems to be the most likely outcome. Perhaps there are too many influences for one young, and sometimes not so young, mind to handle. No wonder there is confusion.

It seems the world is continually changing, and expectations one day may be different the next. What is permissible or expected in one part of the country may be different from another.

Family birth order, role, age, and experience are factors to ponder. When one strips away all the unifying and competing elements, what seems to be left as the underlying guiding principles are values. What does an individual value the most in life? Values come from good and bad people, places, and things. Much is absorbed differently from person to person, even though they may be central to race, culture, era, or nation. Labeling values right or wrong, good or bad is mostly mislabeling.

The interpretation of evil or good may hinge on whether a decision produces terrible or functional outcomes and how those results resonate beyond the individual. Decisions, whether value-based or not, are made by individuals or groups of individuals, but often they have repercussions beyond the individual's or group's circumstances and era.

There was a time, perhaps in my youth (at least, I would like to blame it on my childhood), when I was into my own world, when I did not think much about matters beyond my simple circumstances. I am hardly blaming others for misplaced values just because suddenly I want to think of myself as more enlightened. However, this values thing has been creeping into my mind lately as a big deal. Why do I want to refer to them as misplaced? Is it a generational issue? Who lost them? Were they ever firmly placed? Am I out of step?

No one could have misplaced them if they did not have a place in the first place. And if values are not where I expect them, maybe I am assuming based on my values. Perhaps my rigidness leaves me out of step.

When I hear someone say, "I will call you tomorrow" and then turn around and say, "I will understand if you do not call," I am a little confused. To me, those two things are not the same. I did not hear anywhere in the statement that I would not be getting a call, so what am I missing? Some of my younger friends hear the same comment and say they know where he is coming from, so why am I confused?

I can't say there was a time when all values were the same and people said what they meant and meant what they said, but I am learning how to deal with full-grown adults who don't mean anything they say and don't say anything they mean. It seems values are coming and going as people come and go. It is still a little perplexing. While our values moved and sorted so much, excuse me, why do I feel something is misplaced? Or is it me who's out of place in this skewed valued world?

Peerless

Peer pressure is so powerful all its subjects are immediate victims, powerless, and without recourse. I am going on the record, stating, "That is a view that is widely held and fashionable but ridiculous."

My challenge to everyone, especially teenagers, feeling that is the case when it comes to peer pressure is, do not believe the hype. If you are empowering peer pressure and think you are a victim, let me suggest that this is your opportunity to shine. When what you say matters enough to elicit force from another person, it means you matter. If you are pressured, one way or another, into doing or saying something that is counter to your internal compass, it is a good indication you have an inner compass. You have a conscience—a guide to which you are connected. Understand that is the position from which all greatness flows.

The more you can be true to your internal compass and your beliefs, the more comfortable you will become with who you are and the better you will become at standing up and standing alone without feeling alone. As you begin to feel better about you, who you are and what you stand for, which was maybe previously unbeknownst to you, right before your very eyes and the eyes of the world, you are growing up, maturing, and beginning to take on the traits of someone exceptional. You got that something that all leaders have. You are the one with the pressure, and all along, you thought you were receiving pressure. Many will criticize you for your strength. Don't be unnerved. Remember, the only taste of success some people ever get is when they are taking a bite out of you, so says Zig Ziglar, motivational speaker and author of *See You at the Top*. Lastly, peerless resemblances that other peer-busting word *fearless*.

Stuttering Made Simple

After living with a condition for over fifty years, I finally concluded that if I was born with it, I should investigate it a little deeper. My failure to embrace it earlier may have added to my pain growing up.

Wikipedia describes *stuttering* as "a speech disorder with disrupted speech flow notated by involuntary silent pauses, syllables, words, or phrases as well as spontaneous silent pauses or blocks where the person is unable to produce sounds." Robert West, a pioneer of genetic studies in stuttering, suggested it is because the articulated speech was the last major acquisition in human evolution.

A 2010 article listed three genes correlated with stuttering: GNPTAB, GNPTG, and NAGPA. Researchers estimated that alterations in these three genes were present in 9 percent of people who have a family history of stuttering. The recorded history of stuttering dates to Demosthenes (384–322 BC), who became one of the most prominent Greek statesmen and an orator of ancient Athens after he overcame childhood stuttering. The Talmud interprets Bible passages to indicate Moses was also a stutterer. One common misconception listed in Wikipedia about stuttering is a belief that stutterers cannot be successful. King George VI and Winston Churchill are two world leaders who are said to struggle with stuttering.

Stuttering is typically a developmental disorder beginning in early childhood and continuing into adulthood at some level in at least 20 percent of affected children. It affects 5 percent of the population, and it is relatively consistent across cultures and nationalities where it is measured. Males tend to be affected two to five times more than females. Due to a 65 to 75 percent rate of early recovery, the overall prevalence of stuttering amounts to a low percentage of the population. The portion of stuttering between the races not attributed to economic disparities is small.

My earlier childhood was fraught with rejections, strife, frustration, anger, and bitterness toward any and everything I thought had anything to do with me being different. I even blamed the weather in cases where I thought the cold had something to do with my speech. The number of things stuttering affected negatively in my lifetime from social, psychological, occupational, emotional, economical, and all those in between are unthinkable and immeasurable. My intense desire to hide from the world eventually was overcome by my determination not to be ignored by the world, especially at the honor of those operating from ignorance.

In closing, a condition that represents nearly 5 percent of the population makes it a rare find. Most things that are rare are like gold, exceptionally valuable. However, it was pointed out to me as something unfortunate and sad. I have come to believe it is God's blessing in plain sight, undetectable by many claiming to be intelligent.

Survive or Thrive

In Abraham Maslow's hierarchy of needs, he listed the physical requirements of life as the first and most important of five stages of needs for human survival. There is no motivation to focus on other needs if the essential needs are unmet. Included within the physical phase of requirements are food, shelter, and water.

In some regions of the world, these basic needs are under constant threat. Daily life circumstances test this resilience to do the right thing in various walks of life. Is doing the right thing a guarantee that one will thrive instead of just survive? How can I refuse drug money when not taking it means I have no place to stay, I cannot put food on the table, or my water and lights will be turned off? These dilemmas cloud real character and integrity.

There are documentations of people eating other people to survive. Women, not known for such acts, have sold their bodies to feed their children. Sometimes those of us unfamiliar with such harsh circumstances and choices are quick to judge without offering solutions that account for desperate times. Some are quick to say, "I would never do something that shameful no matter what I am facing." It usually comes from those fortunate enough to have never been tested.

It is true the lack of experience with harsh times camouflages fortitude. It also confuses what one would do with what one wishes he or she would do. To habitually avoid doing the right thing ultimately defines one's fate and says a lot about one's character. The adage, "Tough times don't last; tough people do" is partially correct. Weak people also last, either in the same or in diminished state. It is not just the individual whose fate is affected by one's choices but those currently connected to that individual.

Some simplify such fates as natural outcomes of poor decisions, excuse making, or laziness, while others cite difficult ongoing circumstances as by-products of choices. Maybe it is the people not learning from mistakes or is okay with current conditions. Is it proof that they do not want anything better for themselves? If it is an inherited truth, it is now their situation to keep or dismiss, so tough cookie. If they continue to wallow in it, they own it. Is this the only truth, or is it just another confirmation that Maslow's quest to survive is more complicated than most imagine?

Making one unfortunate choice after another creates flawed truths in the mind of the individual. That reality is passed to the future generations to adopt or reject. The reset button gets harder to find for each generation.

Judgment by observers with power and no connection to such experiences only adds gas to the fire if they claim expertise in the matter. This ultimately serves as a lost opportunity for the expert to learn from someone with a different experience than his at the cross-roads of survive or thrive.

I suspect those living in crime-infected or disassembled communities do not consider it a privilege worth defending. Without an adequate way out, holding on is the preference by default and an effort to save face.

The problem with focusing on surviving, even if it is a condition driven or confirmed by Maslow's hierarchy of needs, is that it makes survival the goal, and it leaves no room for a level of accomplishment beyond just getting by. It creates a mindset of struggle and attachment to survival that makes mediocrity and complacency hard-fought rewards. Letting go of the familiar can be tough. The person who believes this is all he has will fight desperately. Fighting for poverty makes sense when it has been the most dependable companion for years.

When one is challenged continuously by the fight to survive, survival becomes the barrier to thriving. If one is doing everything possible to keep their head above water, it is tough to wrap their head around the concept of getting out of the water. Where stagnation leads, breeds, and lives, progress cannot root or grow.

Martin Luther King Jr. once said, "Only when it's dark enough can you see the stars." One's history must have included at least a glimmer of light from similar dark situations to understand the truth in that statement.

A belief in the hope of moving forward is necessary to take a chance on getting beyond just surviving. Situations that build character and a higher purpose come through difficult and challenging times.

Creating a victory mindset is the goal. We are talking about moving a person to self-actualization, the fifth and final stage of Maslow's hierarchy of needs, while the person is barely maintaining the necessary physical requirements of the first step.

To move one from survival to thrive mode, we must tap into what has been trapped or wiped out by generational constraints. We must loosen up that grip on survival without increasing fear. We need to get the person to let go of the inner tube and take a chance at grasping the boat even though the tube is a family heirloom.

The Institutionalization of Mankind

On the one hand, it is a good thing; on the other, it is not so good. The good is that it allows a man to operate in an orderly and structured manner with rules that benefit the group and the individuals. It also promotes the formulations of other institutions and creates a forum for cooperation and progression that may not be possible without institutionalization.

On the other hand, it burdens individualism and freedom by the subordination of focus from individual thinking. The good of the group is the mission. Sometimes institutional men lose sight of the value and importance of unique and personal matters when concentrating on what's best for the institution.

Solvable Challenge?

Whenever there is a disproportionate accumulation of people in one sector of the population, such as prisons, colleges, hospitals, projects, gated communities, or certain occupations, we must look at the driving forces or policies affecting that outcome. Accidents do not adequately account for certain predictable sizeable patterns of racial and ethnic demographic changes over such a long time. There is usually some level of behind-the-scene manipulation.

The skewed application of the GI bill that was designed to provide housing to veterans in the early twenty-first century resulted in the amassing of wealth in the hands of one race. It was not a happenstance. Unraveling centuries of planned discrimination will not be possible in a short period or without a seismic shift in resources and a commitment over a long term.

The history of solving difficult racial and ethnic problems in this country is to start and then abandon when the pressures of staying the course become too painful to those usually best at inflicting pain. This challenge is an extremely tall order, more in the realm of aspirational and wishful thinking. Americans are also not particularly good at retreating from tall orders when it serves America's interest. Since miracles never cease, it is quite possible this challenge, properly categorized, is achievable if for once, staying the course results in staying the course.

Chapter 4

More Than a Job

Call to Duty

While working as a programmer for the Department of Corrections, I was asked to put together a men's club to give the inmates an opportunity to establish a group of leaders. It would consist of seven to nine members, including a president/treasurer, vice president, and secretary. They were allowed to raise funds for specific projects, such as adopting a homeless family for Christmas, sponsoring a child in a third world country, or purchasing a special dessert or meat to be served to the inmates on a special occasion or holiday. They would also get to submit an article to the local papers, after review, of course, to help inform the public of their leadership and pursuit of excellence.

I felt like this could be a big deal, and if successful, it could become a model for other inmate groups around the state to showcase their talents, rehabilitative potential, and teamwork for good causes. I determined that the president of the club would also serve as treasurer and be responsible for finances. I was to serve as the club's adviser and mediator on the overall management of projects and ideas. It was my job to review the nominees for officers. I was especially interested in who they selected for president. I had veto powers over any nominee.

I spoke with the group of nominees and outlined precisely what the program director and superintendent were looking for and hoping to accomplish. When they presented their choices for president, I immediately dismissed two of them and explained to them that they must be trying to get me fired. I should have known from their opening attempts that this project might not go very well. I did finally settle on a nominee, I thought he would be excellent for what we were trying to do because of how calm, poised, and uncontaminated he appeared. I also thought he had the strength to stand up to attempts by others within the group that might want to push an agenda counter to the long-term interest of the men's club.

The inmates could sell candy, sodas, and other refreshments during visitation as long as they were in self-contained wrappers or containers. It went well and with a strict inventory of what went out and what came in. Officers monitored the count and signed off on the amount received. The president, secretary, and I maintained a copy of the deposit tickets. All went well for the first month.

The inmates pitched an idea to me to allow them to take pictures during the visitation of family and friends. It would require a consent from the family member and a staff witness. The inmates advised that this was an idea that originated from several family members. I had my reservations about this project, and I voiced them to the club. I advised them that I would present it to my supervisors along with my tickets. I was informed to let it proceed with strict monitoring. There is something about inherent criminality that supersedes all conventional wisdom. Right under my eyes and with the apparent consent of the president, I okayed it.

The inmates concocted a grand scheme to sell and trade nude pictures of one another, one another's family members, female friends, and any other female acquaintances who were willing to pose and sell their photos to inmates throughout the compound. This plan was so sophisticated that female accomplices used the same make and model number of the Polaroid we had. Cameras and films were swapped without anyone noticing. Inmates from other areas of the prison got in on the scheme and sent naked or near-naked poses to the visitation area to be sold or traded.

They had enough extra unaccounted film for a replacement to maintain accurate inventory down to every mistake and blurry shot. Only a stroke of luck for me uncovered the scheme. In the inmate's haste to exchange and account for film, one inmate left a shot in the camera that did not automatically eject. It did, however, take and develop fully. It revealed unauthorized organs and body parts usually only viewed during strip searches. The program terminated. All club members and other inmates found in collusion were locked up. It was my understanding that they were working on expanding the operation to include smuggling photos from nearby prisons.

Charles in Charge

Reflecting on my first day on the job as a correction officer brought with it some very memorable, unnerving moments. Fresh out of college, with no orientation to speak of, I was instructed to report to C-block to shadow Officer Jackson. I had a uniform, but I had no name tag. So I had to tell him my name. As luck would have it, I was not by his side two minutes before Mr. Jackson got a call to direct me to B-block to replace that officer because he went on a road trip. When I reported to Officer Jackson, he was completing some paperwork, so he never got the opportunity to explain anything to me. So I still had no idea what I was supposed to do. Instead of shadowing someone, I would oversee running a block.

When I got upstairs to B-block, the officer I was supposed to relieve had already left, so there was no one to brief me about that block. The officer running the area between A and B blocks handed me a bunch of keys. I had no idea to what they belonged. He said, "You are going to be working down here" as he pointed in the direction of B-block. I was not sure he knew my name. Then the phone started ringing, so he opened the door and shoved me on B-block so he could pick up the phone. I guess he did not have time to tell me anything either.

B-block was a ward with about eight or nine rooms. It had eight to ten inmates per room. The rooms had double bunk beds. There were about eighty inmates assigned to that block at the time. I stepped on the block and watched the officer hurry away. I was a little nervous, but I did not want the inmates to know. I tried to stand erect and step with confidence. I got about an eighth of the way down the hall when an inmate approached me. He said, "You are?"

I said, "Calhoun, why you want to know?" I tried to say it with a little bass and force, although my knees were shaking a little.

He said, "So you are Officer Calhoun, Mr. Calhoun."

I said, "Yes, that's right."

Since I have a speech impediment that seems to act up badly when I am nervous, I was in perhaps my worst predicament. I tried to pause every time he said something to gather myself so I would not stutter. I also attempted to keep my answers to one or two words.

There were concession machines in the hallway with sodas and other snacks. The inmate said, "My name is Charles." Now he stood about five feet five. He was probably a little under a buck fifty, maybe one of the smallest guys on the block and one of the few guys I was larger than. He said, "Listen, Mr. Calhoun, Officer Calhoun, what do you want us to call you because I see you don't have a name tag yet?"

I said, "Go ahead."

"Like I was saying, I am Charles, and I run all this down here," he said as he pushed a guy back who went about six feet six, 265 pounds, all muscles. By that time, I was surrounded by about ten inmates. He told them, "Y'all back up and give Officer Calhoun some room."

They all said, "Yes, sir, Mr. Charles."

He went on to say, "Where was I? If you have any problems down here, you just come see me, I will take care of it for you. But listen here, Mr. Calhoun, did they not tell you what was customary for all the new officer to do for the inmate in charge on the block?"

I said, "No."

He said, "Well, you are supposed to buy the inmate in charge a soda and a nab. Now I will take a Mountain Dew, and it doesn't matter what kind of nab you get me."

"I don't want to break the custom, but let me talk to the other officer in the center before I do that."

He said, "You don't have to do that, Mr. Calhoun. Ain't that right, guys?" They all nodded in agreement. "I wouldn't jive on anything like that, Mr. Calhoun, because we are going to be working down here together. We got to take care of each other."

I said, "Well, I would still like to check with the officer anyway."

"Well, if you insist, be my guest," he said as he cleared a path for me to walk through.

I asked the officer in the center about the custom, and he snatched me off the block and berated me about entertaining that garbage. He said, "Them inmates don't tell you shit to do. I know to what Charles you are referring. That little bastard needs to go somewhere and sit his ass down before I have you and him locked up. You sure you are a college graduate? Don't you come back out here with no more of them inmates' bullshit either."

I thought to myself, *No one has told me anything about what I should do, but I am getting raked over the coals on what I should not do.* I did not know staff talked that way to other staff members. Was he serious about having me locked up too? The only thing I had been told thus far had come from an inmate in charge and a pissed off staff member. I was feeling a little uneasy on both sides of the door. I was not sure who was safer to be around. When I went back on the block, they had all scattered and were in their rooms. Charles did come back out and say, "I was just funning, Mr. Calhoun. We were just playing around. I won't be going to let you spend money on me unless you want to do."

I told him, "You and I do not have any more to say to each other. You need to go on about your business, okay?"

"O…kay, Mr. Officer. Drive on."

As embarrassing as it was, my experience that day with Charles taught me more about dealing with inmates than I would have probably got from Officer Jackson all day. I could not believe I fell for the inmate in charge's stunt and asked an officer about such a silly custom. It was jailhouse/prison 101—old-school style. They broke me in hard and swift. From that point forward, I got it.

Incident of Unextreme Probation

My work as a probation officer presented some awkward and exciting scenarios. I suppose some of the events had a lot to do with the cast of diverse characters with whom I worked: Wiley, Deron, Sandy, Millicent, Latonya, Hornsby, Teresa, Keith, and Conrad. Although many of the probation officers were former military, law enforcement, and corrections officials, I found the work environment just as comical as it was serious.

Although this was the one job I ascribed to when I got out of college, I found it was not exactly suited to my skill set. The position had become more paperwork than the community and field work I expected. My chief, Conrad, initially reminded me he was a computer whiz and so adept that he could fix any computer problem. He just wanted me to enter cases to the best of my ability. After about three months of my ineptness, my screwups had him so baffled that he told me to forget everything he said before I gave him another stroke. In the end, he credited me for increasing his computer skill level tremendously. Come to think of it, I never got paid for that.

I did work hard, but I never learned to enter cases with the fluency of some officers, such as Millicent or Deron. To be truthful, I did not learn to register them with fluency comparable to anyone, except maybe Ms. Tew; we may had been neck and neck.

I am still not convinced that Deron's unique modus operandi wasn't south of the law, especially after he invoked a line from the movie *Top Gun*: "If I tell you, then I would have to kill you." With this character, he could have been serious.

One time, my court partner Teresa's desk mysteriously got turned around and flipped upside down like the life of *The Fresh Prince of Bel-Air*. Her resulting kangaroo-style investigation nabbed fellow officer Wiley, not as a suspect but the culprit unequivocally. To this day, I do not know who ramp-shacked her office, but the case is closed, too hot to touch and too cold for CSI.

Now Wiley could be a jokester, but my first encounter with him involved especially important business—his flashlight. Wiley's torch resembled a Louisville Slugger more than it did a flashlight, so my

first question was, where did he get it or where can I get one? I figured Dirty Harry needed to share the wealth, although after handling
it, I found it a little too cumbersome. He said it was an illuminating
device. I immediately wondered if Wiley was referring to it producing light for the probation officers or stars for the probationers. I did
not want to inspect its intention much closer in case he was thinking
about providing me a little demonstration.

Later I was given a hint of Wiley's modus operandi when he
reminded a quietly sitting probationer that he had two choices before
him: straight to the county jail or to the jailhouse by way of the
hospital. The probationer and I were both startled by Wiley's infer-
ence that he expected trouble from a guy who presented himself as
the poster child for humbleness. Now sometimes heavy hands were
required in our line of work, but this case did not warrant it unless
Wiley was privy to information I didn't have.

In another incident, an officer pepper-sprayed a dog and docu-
mented that he had to walk to the other side of the porch where the
dog was sleeping to pepper spray it. He claimed it was for his peace
of mind. He had to secure his blind side. He further stated he did not
know what the dog was up to; perhaps it was just playing possum. To
be fair, our training was a little short on reading the minds of dogs,
so maybe the officer was at a disadvantage. Aren't we all sort of always
unsure about the intentions of dogs?

Seeing how I seem to be only able to recall some of the lighter
and comical moments of the days and life of a probation officer,
you might think we coddled and didn't supervise and revoke our
probationers and parolees. There was one occasion when a parolee
who had absconded five years earlier angered one of his in-laws who
dropped a dime on him, and like clockwork, when he returned with
his daughter from Florida, he was easy pickings. I thanked him for
having a big mouth and told him he might need a refresher to his
anger-management program. I will let the probationers and the
parolees tell the rest of their stories. I am sure if they elect to put a
positive spin on it, it would be received as much more genuine than
any version I could tell.

Just Shoot Me

I have heard a lot of things in life that I might classify as crazy. I imagine you have had your share of them. But there is one thing that stands out as one of my most bizarre.

While working as a corrections officer, I was privy to witness a gathering of inmates doing what they called spitting the truth. As I moved closer and zoomed in on the conversation, I realized that one inmate had the floor. He was advising his fellow inmates how to get shot in the head and survive. As he talked, more inmates gathered around. Inmates were calling other inmates to hear his story. So he had to repeat it more than once. He said, "This is what you do." I thought to myself, *How about telling them how to avoid getting shot?* "Well, first when a guy pulls down on you, square up and look him in the eyes. Then you turn to the side to give your shooter a thinner target to hit." *Wait a minute, isn't he about two feet from the shooter?* "Now if you can, put your heart on the side opposite of him. That would be better. You see, you don't want to give him a major organ if you can help it," he said. I guess he was telling the guy had such a lousy shot that he might not even hit the head. Maybe he thought the lungs are not a primary organ or perhaps the ribs are stronger on the side opposite the heart. He had my attention. I thought this was going to be good. He started out telling people how to get shot in the head. Now he was schooling them with a bonus on how to take a body shot, I guess, just in case the shooter chooses to kill you softly. I was getting confused, but I figured I might as well hear him out. I thought I might learn something from this character. On the occasion that I choose to shoot myself, at least I will not have to learn the hard way which organs to avoid.

I do not think I will ever need his information other than sharing the bizarreness with others. I also hope his fellow inmates do not go out looking for an opportunity to get shot either.

Well, he did bring his conversation back to the head. He said, "Turn to the side, keep your arm tight to your side, and raise and hunch your shoulders as high as you can just in case he fires lower than he is aiming. You know it is always better to take the shot in the arm or high shoulder if you can. You want to try to bait him into making that shot in the arm if it is possible." *Does he want you to get a little cozy with your executioner?* He continued, "You know, almost as you do with a dog, I mean, K-9; you give it your arm instead of a vital body part." I did not think any of those were exposed unless the pants were sagging too low at the wrong time. I thought, *Now he is giving a lesson on how to deal with an attack dog.* I was beginning to think this guy was an all-around expert in taking on crime—dummy style. I was waiting for him to show us his teeth marks and then explain how he kept his ears out of harm's way. But anyway, he said, "Before a person shoots you or before the gun goes off, there is a snap before the pistol fires, so you have to keep your eyes on the gun. When you hear that snap, you immediately throw your head back slightly so when the bullet hits your head, your head is angled backward in such a way that it causes the bullet to glance instead of going straight through. You must fall back immediately and remain still as if you are dead." He then said, "I am telling you all this because that is what I did. You see, I am still here."

I decided to check his file a little closer to see if there was anything about this shooting. I could see a mark on his forehead, but that could be from many other things, including a bullet. It turned out it was true that he got shot in the head. However, there were some things, important things, he left out. This tough guy failed to mention anything about spending three weeks in intensive care with two of them in a coma. When macho man fell backward after being shot, he probably was not playing dead. He most likely was unconscious. He also did not mention he got shot with a small caliber .25 semiautomatic, the so-called Saturday night special, an inexpensive, low-quality, junk gun. It was not exactly the kind of firearm from which one would expect maximum damage. Not that a .25 will not kill you, but had it been a .44 magnum or even a .357, I do not think I would have ever known about his story, at least, not with him telling it. How much turning his body to the side and snapping the head backward actually contributed to his survival is highly questionable. I would instead think that God was smiling on this idiot of a soul and that he would do well to place the credit there and leave it. Those who want to take his advice and go out and challenge someone to "Just shoot me" might want to tell their story before they do it. I do not think they are going to get to do the part where they play dead.

Shields

When we think of a protector or defender of something, we think of a shield. Since I am referring to one of our superintendents of the prison where I worked, I guess he could be considered the top shield. The number 1 responsibility of the prison employees, regardless of their position, was the protection of the public, staff, inmates, and state property, and in that order. He made sure all his team understood that the public was not going to be unsecured under his watch due to inept security practices.

Mr. Shields came to Hoke Correctional Institution from Caledonia State Prison Farm. Caledonia had initially been a 7500-acre work farm that housed maximum-security male inmates. Caledonia, at one time, briefly housed females on the top floor and males on the bottom. It opened for occupancy in 1892. It is currently, at this writing, a male medium custody unit.

Shields, who came up through the ranks of security from a corrections officer to the top unit commander, brought his rough and tough brand of correction with him. It did not take long to rub staff and inmates the wrong way. Loud and boisterous, often he walked up and down the hall barking orders loud enough to wake up the dead.

Once while entering the dining area, he overheard an inmate complaining about a lockdown at Shield's facility being worse than the farm. In short order, he had that inmate jerked out of the dining line. Shields shouted that the inmate was on his way to the farm and that he would be picking tomatoes tomorrow. "Anybody wants to go with him?" barked Shields. He was so loud that when he called staff into his office and closed the door, staff members three entries down would be scrambling for earplugs.

I had to go to his office once for writing a scorching letter to the Area Office Interview Review Board in advance of an interview. I

berated the interviewers and cited the process as so flawed and wasteful that even crooks would appreciate the ruse. He was so shocked
that I wrote such a letter that he tapered his wrath with a statement
of understanding about my frustration. He said that was the wrong
platform to vent my annoyance. Since I attacked the character of
the interviewers, some of whom I did not know, he instructed me to
send them a letter of apology.

F-block was a twenty-four-person, single-cell unit with twelve
cells on each side with an activity quarter in the center. One day as
Mr. Shields left the facility to go home, inmates on F-block facing
the parking lot, where staff left the prison, shouted obscenities to
him. They included that he was a slick back, greasy head, and Jheri
curl faggot and, of course, a few other things too vulgar to mention. I
do not know if he had any place to go after work. If so, it had to wait.
He made a U-turn and was on the unit in a matter of minutes. "Who
said that!" he shouted. "You are all yellow-bellied punks if you can't
repeat it to my face." Of course, he got no takers. They might have
been yellow-bellied punks, but they were not dumb yellow-bellied
punks. Then he said, "Open these doors. I want every swinging dick
on this side moved to the other side." An inmate called Sweet Thing
stepped out of his cell and said, "I got mine tied up, boss man."

"Untie his dick and move his ass to the other side with the other
eleven cowards. I might not know who hollered at me," said Shields,
"but your view from now on will be the woods. The only thing you
will be hollering at tomorrow will be squirrels and raccoons. Now let
me hear something else from you, and you will be 'smelling gas' [a
reference that an inmate's transfer is imminent] in the prison van on
your way to Caledonia or some other place where it will take your
Mama months to visit you."

Some thought Mr. Shields was irritable, ill-tempered, and can-
tankerous; but I found him to be fair—an equal-opportunity abuser.
Those who slithered under and away from the rules and the laws of
the main shield of the public by calling him something other than his
name found this "shield" loaded with shrapnel.

Work Ethic, Anyone?

Recently, I had a conversation with an employer who expressed frustration with a flood of applicants who thought mentioning work ethic in connection with employment was unnecessary. He said, "Can you believe the employee remarked, 'What does my work ethic have to do with me preparing a line for lunch?'" He went on to ask, "How can someone cop an attitude with an employer about such a matter but still expect the employer to rate him high?"

As an employer myself, I share some of this employer's aggravation. I have never included that question in my interview process. I can see how it can become significant if suddenly work ethic is missing in every employee. Wikipedia has a lot to say about the phrase, so perhaps those looking to land that ideal job may want to brush up on the meaning. Work ethic is a value based on hard work and diligence. It is also a belief in the moral benefit of work and its ability to enhance character. An example would be the Protestant work ethic. A work ethic may include being reliable, having initiative, or pursuing new skills.

Workers exhibiting a good work ethic, in theory, should get better positions, more responsibility, and ultimately promoted. Workers who fail to display a good work ethic are failing to provide fair value for the wage the employer is paying them and should not get positions of greater responsibility.

I guess a potential applicant who only wishes to prepare a line for lunch would not be interested in a promotion or higher responsibility. To quiz such an employee about matters not causally related to the skill set needed for a specific job may be considered out-of-bounds by such a person.

Let me add this to Wikipedia: those with no concept of work ethic would be most expendable or the first fired. Now considering work ethic when reviewing an employee's resume is not illegal, and it indeed should not be viewed as offensive unless living up to such an ethic when it comes to work is just too much to ask.

Chapter 5

Substance

And the Winner Is...

I should not have to tell you who the losers are. It may be applicable around the world, but I am going to focus on America. I decided to write this after talking to my cousin Roscoe. I asked him what made him stop drinking. He said, "I sat down one day and told myself I have been drinking for many years, and you know, alcohol never did anything for me. I am going to stop doing things for it. So I put it down and have not picked it up in over a year."

His story is unique. Not many reach the same conclusion. There appears to be unlimited resourcefulness and commitments to getting high. Americans love their alcohol and drugs. Our wealth and popularity as a nation camouflage the severity of the problem. An example is how the wealth of a rich person conceals drug use so his issues are not immediately apparent, while the poor man's lights and gas are turned off.

Because Americans have money and an overinflated ego and a sense of invincibility, the first country every dealer wants to market drugs is America. Why wouldn't they? Ever heard a fool and his money are soon parted? We think we are too rich, too important, and much too smart and powerful for it to be a concern. It is a recipe for maximum exploitation. How do I know the drug problem in America will get worse? Americans are the problem. Drugs are just a vehicle tailor-made for the maximum exploitation of our egotistical flaws.

When we think we know everything or know what is best but continue to be bitten by the same dog and imagine our money and standing in the world as the solution to everything, we are destined for trouble. We are the masters of freedom, conquerors of the universe. Who among us can tell us what to do? Indeed, no outsider is going to tell us what to do.

I see the money flowing into the latest drug epidemic—opioids. Anyone believing this is a crisis due to underfunding and thinking more money will solve it is a part of that bandwagon of nonsense why the drug dealers love America. The dealers will even capitalize on the money that is poured into treatment.

Imagine the drug problem is cured. Americans would not stand around and not get high. We would go to the laboratories and invent something. We are inventors and too ingenious to live a boring life. We have too much money, too much time, and too little sense to think a life without being high is worth living. Even our freedom to the pursuit of happiness is tied up in the freedom to use drugs. See if you can remember the last celebration you attended that did not include drugs or the promise of drugs later. Those who opt out are called squares, not even worthy of being called Americans. It is the ultimate peer pressure.

Alcohol and drugs have consistently provided deceit, distortion, and a false sense of courage and confidence. Nothing about the use of alcohol or drugs that outweighs its destruction has been worthy of passing from one generation to the next. However, no other family heirloom I can think of has enjoyed more presence at more family gatherings. There is an unwritten promise that it will be there for every age to come. Prohibition was our fight for that right. Yes, some died for the cause.

Let me return to my cousin's comment. I know by now he does not expect alcohol and drug to repay him for all his loyalty and commitment. The fact that a lot of drug use is legal (alcohol and over-the-counter and prescribed drugs), it guarantees you as an unsuspecting candidate for exploitation and abuse.

We are past the point where the effect of drugs and alcohol surprises people. Every family knows a member's life that has been ruined. The numbers who have been laid to waste, famous and infamous, are a part of drug's and alcohol's history for all to see. There is nothing new about this new opioid crisis. But there is something of which I am sure: we will choose more drugs and alcohol. The Lord knows it to be true, and the drug lords know it to be true.

Faulty Thinking

Two things I think would serve some significantly are independent and sound thinking and staying away from alcohol and drugs. Denying oneself of alcohol and drugs will not guarantee the first one, but not staying away from alcohol and drugs will significantly diminish the effort to be an independent and sound thinker.

Since many subtle things in life affect thinking, such as political affiliation, religion, tradition, and culture, it is complicated to know how independent and sound one's thought is. We have become polarized by being a part of a society that gently and continuously forces one to choose a position of thinking that is favorable or opposed to specific groups and subjects. Current thinking may be the result of an individual's phase in life. In certain areas of the world and during specific eras, changing loyalties has amounted to excommunication or extermination. Deviations, even occasionally, may be perceived as splitting loyalties, which may be unforgiveable.

Certain divisions amounted to successions and prompted the American Civil War when southern states joined South Carolina and decided against the Union rather than fight their neighbors after shots were fired at the battle of Fort Sumter.

Anytime one decides to take off as a lone wolf in thinking, it is a good chance it is foolish or wise. Depending on which, it may prove costly if economics are tied to those loyalties.

It is rarely initially seen as honorable to buck the power structure, tradition, or the status quo even when the motive is noble, such as standing for justice as Nelson Mandela did against apartheid. Jesus's position was against the power structure of his times.

The question is, Is it better to stand on principle and be dishonored and not accepted or to be liked or accepted and continue to be a part of the team?

The fault of thinking with loyalties means the truth is blotted out when being a team player carries more significance. It is often the case in politics. Clouded perceptions about thinking and positions muddy the truth, contaminate individual responsibilities, and create situations where the value of facts is so weak it is not a factor in the outcome.

Independent and sound thinking is a choice. It involves an enormous personal battle within each person's consciousness. Countless take the easy way out. It's spurned many phrases, such as "don't rock the boat," "don't bite the hand that feeds you," "blood is thicker than water," "go with the flow," and "either you are with us or against us."

Many are referred to as snitches if they break ranks. They may pay for it with their lives or become living proof that snitches get stitches. Independent and sound thinking is not without peril.

A mind is compromised when it is tainted with alcohol and other drugs. It is incapable of clear and individual thought, let alone as a part of a group. In a crowd, its compromised state is multiplied. It is often pointless to continue challenging binding conclusions of a group for which one chooses. In other words, arguing with a drunk is dumb; arguing with a bunch of drunks is dumber.

To uproot faulty thinking, it requires judgment and the willingness to live with the consequences. Alcohol and other drugs double down on an already-exhausting process. It all but guarantees that independent and sound thinking will be faulty.

Prescription Madness

According to IMS Health Vector One National database in 2013, 8,389,034 kids were on psychiatric drugs in the United States. The age breakdown is 1,274,804 children from birth to one year old and 370,778 for children between two and three years of age. For children aged four to five, there were 500,948. The largest number belonged to children aged six to twelve, which was 4,130,340. For children aged between thirteen and seventeen, there were 3,617,593.

A November 2008 article by Andrew M. Weiss, "The Wholesale Sedation of America's Youth," listed approximately 7,500 children diagnosed with mental disorders in the United States in 1950. That would be an over 1,100 percent increase over sixty years.

As I tiptoe in this venture, I want to advance a theory. I want to start by either dismissing or accepting the physiological or biological nature of children as it relates to behavior. Behaviors have so radically changed from 1950 to the present that it justifies such an increase in medication or something is amiss. If true, the scientific community is grossly derelict in not seeing it coming. It should have been labeled as a pending pandemic.

There are some chronically neurological and mental ill children in this country, but to jump from seven thousand to eight million in sixty years, where sixty years before 1950 provided no trend, is concerning.

How to best improve aberrant behavior in a free society in the least restrictive manner is a legitimate subject to deliberate. Many interests have formulated fixed positions. Biases are neutralized or blinded, especially where livelihoods and entire industries are at stake. Supporting facts are also manipulated to highlight the many competing interests.

So what does account for the increase, and how did we get here? The first Diagnostic Statistical Manual (DSM-I) was published in 1952. It listed one childhood disorder: adjustment reaction of childhood/adolescence. Children were expected to be rambunctious, and parents were supposed to monitor and guide.

The pharmaceutical industry operates within a capitalistic system where profit and shareholders' interests are paramount. There are many economic interests that are interrelated. Also, there are many socially disconnected sectors working in an arena where checks and balances would be counter to market goals. Stakeholders with enough knowledge to challenge the pharmaceutical industry are offering counternarratives on a social and moral platform. Perhaps some represent the interests of mental-health constituents who viewed mental-health clients as lower class and sometimes throw-aways. At first glance, the documentation of horrific procedures perpetrated by the psychiatry industry in the mental asylums in the early to mid-twentieth century in the name of medicine suggested certain things were only available to this population. Is there anyone minding the henhouse?

Chapter 6

❖

Fair Play

A Contract Is a Contract

It is a situation concerning a contractual arrangement that I will try to explain without revealing particulars. Recently, I had a front-row seat in some of the most brazen shenanigans that I have ever witnessed. It is not that I haven't been around or seen trickery before, but the level of this was beyond comparison.

I can be naive, according to some. I think of myself as genuine and straightforward in my perception of life and people but astute in matters of character and human interaction. I am more apt to think most people are good and tend to want to do the right thing and have a sense of care and concern for their fellow man. Listening to arguments in court caused me to pause on some of my positions on people and their ideas of justice. Is winning the only thing, or is winning more important than anything? If you do not win, do you get any points for being a good sport?

Part of our culture teaches us to play to win, which, for some, is not any different from a win at all cost. This partially explains why star athletes, the ones we find out about, are still willing to risk it all by cheating for the sake of winning. There is a saying that goes something like this: "Show me someone who does not mind losing, and I will show you someone who loses often." Winners hate to lose, and losers rarely win. So if you don't play to win, you should not play at all. At least that seems to be the principal school of thought.

When it involves a person's chosen profession, participation in the game is a foregone conclusion, so the option to not play is off the table. Not having the stomach for nastiness subjects you to getting clobbered by those amazingly comfortable with winning at any cost.

I began to see the dentist chair as a beautiful thing. How and why did I get here without committing a crime or without ever being accused of any wrongdoing? I chose to get in the business. I felt like a driver in a bus controlled by others. Not only did I get on the bus freely but I also brought some friends along. All of us invested and sacrificed heavily in time and money. The operator of the vehicle encouraged and even assisted us in obtaining the highest level of training for this journey. Those who committed to the best continuing education and training were preferred. The ride started smoothly. Somewhere on the trip, things changed. A new driver had taken charge, and he changed the rules. He offered no refunds and no explanations. He stated that he was under no obligation to explain and that I had no appeal rights. I was told to get off the bus in three months and that I had signed a contract agreeing to do so. Why was I in court if I agreed to that? Why was I in court contesting an agreement?

It was the second time I had to use the courts. An attempt was made to put me out of the business about three years ago. So I thought, *Here we go again*. After riding the bus for years, I received a letter riddled with enough falsehoods to make Mother Teresa look like Pinocchio. It came from a few hired guns who said, "You have been granted three more months to ride this bus. Should you choose not to sign, your ride will end. Should you decide to sign, your trip will terminate." It sounded like the same deal to me. "Your journey will not renew even though we have not ever seen you or reviewed your case. We provided you with a request for proposal [RFP] that pretty much sealed your fate along with many others because we can do that. You do not have any appeal rights because it would be unfathomable for you to think that you have a right to be in business forever and that we have no power to end a contract especially after it legally expires. If I said you got a fair deal, you got a fair deal. Because you have no rights that I am bound to respect, I am willing to put in writing that even if you scored one hundred on the RFP, I could still put you off the bus because the waiver law gives me that right."

Somewhere I heard that once before, about "having no rights that I am bound to respect." Oh, I know. It was 1857, over one hundred years before I was born, in the Dred Scott v. John F. A. Sandford case. Is it that time flies, or is it the more things change, the more they remain the same? I know there are those who will say I am reaching and my situation in court in no way compares to that of Dred Scott. Certainly not. When others are arguing your fate and you are unintelligent, it is an honor and privilege to have that done. When you are intelligent enough to make sense of the communication, it is like people talking as if you are not in the room. I can make out what they are saying, but I must pretend I do not know what is going on. I know I am screwed by a system and by the horse I rode in.

I was asked to get off the bus in three months and take my friends with me. Then one of the executioners showed up in court without his gun and purported to take the highest moral ground. He said, "Judge, I do apologize for troubling you. I do not know why he is here. He got more than I was required to give him. I mean, the RFP and things he got was much more than he deserves, so I have no idea why he is here. Besides, judge, can you believe he signed a contract saying he would leave? So I think he should abide by the agreement. I am just here to see justice done. You can already see he is not a man of his word because he refuses to honor his contract. I am here to ask you to enforce the contract he signed, your honor. I want you to overlook the fact that I gave him a no-win ultimatum, that I had him over a barrel, and that I still got him over that barrel. Judge, I want you to know I hold all the cards. It may as well be a gun.

"I am honorable, and I always act with the utmost regard for everyone's rights. There is no need to second-guess anything I do. I am fair, infallible, and will still act in the best interest of the little man even though I have a waiver that says I do not have to. Also, I have a couple of big brothers, DHHS and the state legislature, who are monitoring me even though they put me up to this. They pretty much rubber-stamp anything I do. You can count on me to make sure everyone is treated fairly. So, judge, why don't you issue a ruling in my favor, retire to your chambers, and let me handle the debris?

"We have already rounded up most of his friends and put them in shackles. This one is refusing to take his medicine, so it has been a little tricky to put him to sleep. Perhaps, he had a little more money, so the choke hold we put on him did not take him out. Judge, if you would just tell him he doesn't have any rights, we can dismiss with him fairly quickly, and then you can get to the golf course early.

"Besides, judge, you don't have any power over us. I did not want to go there and say this, but you may get hurt, sticking your nose where it does not belong. A contract is a contract, so you need to do what you do best. Enforce this agreement or else I will see you in court, explaining why you refused to do your job, which is pretty much what everyone else does, rubber-stamp our demands. Somebody is feeling their oats!"

A flimflam is an absurdity no matter how well it is polished. Most confuse craftiness, cleverness, and ruthlessness in business with intelligence or acuity. The swiftness and bullying leave little time to check on those smashed to smithereens. It is also the most accurate indication of a downfall. The participants would not know a level playing field if they slept on it. Entitlements, privileges, and superior positions are their ideal playing field; they are quick to surmise that others are unable to compete due to their excellent cerebral skills.

A contract may be more than a contract. Get the slug out your eye and keep peeling back the onion. There is a time when winners are made to rest, some in golden orchards. All decay the same.

Fertile Ground

Occasionally, I am reminded of others and the media about the different discussions centered on inequality and equality in life. There are plenty of good arguments on many sides about the problems with the poor and the problems with the wealthy.

In a country where the constitution guarantees the right to free speech and the pursuit of happiness, the freedom to succeed or fail is in that quest. The law does not ensure the realization of either, just a right to pursue.

An argument with an outcome that confirms a reason to be divided may be reasonable, but it is probably not especially useful if we are trying to find solutions.

Inequality in America is as simple as it is complicated. This country is a tragedy and a triumph, given the fact that it originated with a black man as three-fifths of man and not allowed anywhere near the White House except as a laborer. For eight years, a black man lived in the White House as chief executive.

The nation is a history of people who have risen from some of the most miserable poverty-stricken conditions to some of the wealthiest people in the world. Henry Ford, a pioneer in automaking, is one well-known example. Oprah Winfrey is an African-American journalist who rose from poverty to wealth.

Are race and poverty insignificant barriers? Because such examples break all expectations, sometimes we label those who languished in poverty as shady instead of believable. Some in poverty mark the wealthy as insensitive, greedy, and uncaring. Perhaps, neither of these arguments is right, at least, not entirely.

I want to use myself as an example of what I believe is closer to the truth and a better starting point. I am the product of a reasonably healthy birth, except being a little premature. I did have a severe speech impediment. My upbringing is with illiteracy and miserable poverty. Aside from the obvious physical negatives of the environment, the most crucial element is not apparent—the mental framing or mindset that such a situation produces. What I acquired from my upbringing is central to my community and the era of which I grew up. Neither the rich nor the poor is to blame. I am not seeking to divide and destroy or make any excuses. I just want to expand on what my experiences taught me about the equality and the inequality in our society.

I am sure both my parents loved my siblings and me and wanted the best for us. I am also almost positive they were not fans of poverty nor were they opposed to being wealthy. Some of the core beliefs I acquired from the environment were not accidentally instilled nor were they offered as part of a larger design to hinder my progress.

High school graduation was a must. I believed that was possible. I saw anything beyond high school as out of my reach. I figured college was for other people who were much smarter and more deserving. I believed I should get a job in a local factory. We did not have a car for much of my childhood; I had never been outside of neighboring towns where I was born.

The expectations were to get a job in the local community and enjoy it. I did not have electricity, television, or telephone until my teen years. I had no sense of what this world had to offer. My beliefs were determined by where I lived and to whom I gravitated. At the time, I had no idea that my insight and outlook could be broadened and determined by forces beyond my parents or community. My environment was insufficient. It limited my thinking and belief. Those around me reinforced those limitations, and I, in turn, shared and strengthened them in a loop scenario with other friends outside of my inner circle. It happened so casually.

I would have settled into any job that paid anything. I labored for free for my father for years to put a roof over my head so that minimum-wage job would have been a raise. I believed I should have and deserve no more than a used car, with no extras. I was very hesitant about assuming I should have or want too much because that would be a bad thing and would cause me to begin thinking out of my limits or out of my place. I did not quite know what my place was, but I knew what was out of my league and beyond my reach. I did not want to think uppity.

I remembered one time thinking how awesome it would be to get a double-wide trailer, but then I said to myself, *Quit dreaming. You know a singlewide is where you belong.* This type of thinking permeated my foundation and every function of my life, even down to the girls I thought I should pursue. Now it did not stop me from being attracted to the pretty and popular girls, but I mostly kept those thoughts to myself and wondered what they would want with my stuttering ass. My career choices hinged on those ideas and beliefs.

My lack of early expansive exposure produced a product inconsistent with the content of the product. Inside, I do not know what
or why, but something was discontent. I felt unsettled. I thought I
had to stay true to what I should be and to not bring shame on my
family or community, but there just had to be more than what I
was being led to believe. Every time I slipped up or secretly moved
beyond where I thought I should be, a neighbor or a friend would
call me boy or stupid.

A police officer stopped me while I was driving a Mercedes, and
he asked me what I was doing with that white man's car. I told him
he sold it to me, and he asked me if I was trying to be funny. I was
getting ready to say the white man's name when he cut me off and
asked me for my license and registration.

When I was a corrections officer, a fellow officer and I was jog-
ging in Pinehurst, North Carolina one night. A policeman stopped
us, saying he was responding to a report of a couple of thugs running through the neighborhood. I told him I hadn't seen any. He
instructed me to just answer the question. Being in law enforcement
by that time, I knew that statement was a prelude to massive hands,
so I said, "No, sir." Due to my unsure place in life, my sense of
belonging was always in limbo.

Let me explain the quirky situation that started me believing
outside my family and community limitations. It took the actions of
someone not from my immediate environment or community. On
my senior year in high school, I planned to get a regular job in a local
factory or go in the military, not as a high-ranking officer but maybe
just as one or two ranks above private first class.

A virtual stranger, my school counselor, whom I had never
spoken to before, called me to his office and interrupted my well-
thought-out dream that I got from my loving parents, siblings, and
community. The counselor had the nerve to tell me I needed to go
to college. I was taught to be respectful to my elders and authority,
but I could not help it. I laughed in his face and told him he must
be kidding. I was a good student academically, but high school was
as high as I believed I belonged. I honestly felt something awful was
going to happen to him for playing a prank on me. I thought he was

70

just so funny. I could not believe he was serious. I never bothered telling anyone why the counselor called me to his office.

The sad thing about my situation is not that it happens but that it does not happen enough. Most people in my predicament never have anyone interrupt their grossly ingrain inept dreams. My situation is not unusual; in fact, it is typical of what comes out of the many malnourished communities. It, in my mind, explains the growing inequities. Sure, the system is rigged, the playing field is not level, and the rules are against some.

The most critical factor yielding inequity is thinking. A limited thinker would make no significant use of a system or playing field that is rigged for him or slanted in his favor. The undernourished or poorly fertile grounds from which a class or generation of people emerge account for a significant number of tarnished, subdued, and limited thinkers who populate rolls of poverty, crime, illiteracy, substance dependency, welfare, and the homelessness in the country.

Unfortunately, the longer a person languishes in such an environment, the more difficult it becomes when exposed to someone or something that can help them move beyond where they are. They are mostly shunned by the privileged, thinking they don't want to be bothered. Another factor working against a person in this situation is, the older one gets, the more difficult it is to get them to believe they should have more. Much of the fight and belief has been taken out of them. If you can change a mindset from limited thinking to limitless thinking, then a rigged system with unfair rules and an unlevel playing field become a solvable exercise. The earlier, the better.

Those from the wealthiest of communities who have a history of generational wealth are only exposed to wealth and the more delicate things of life. They have little trouble transcending into more wealth because their expectations and beliefs of what they deserve are consistent with what they have grown up around.

In many cases, the rich have nothing against the poor; they may erringly believe the poor is poor because in their freedom to choose, they made decisions that caused them to be poor like the ones they made that led them to wealth. Unbeknownst to them is the level and grip of the invisible mental framing that accounts for a mindset of poverty thinking that is just as typical as wealth thinking in their circle. It is an unfamiliar area of thought for the rich.

Some families and communities are poised to build generational wealth, while other families and communities are poised to produce generational poverty. Both mindsets produce outcomes consistent with their teachings.

Some persons who get out of impoverishing conditions will acquire an attitude of indifference to the plight of those hemmed in by the mental doggedness of generational poverty. "If I did it, they could do it" is their position.

Years in that predicament without a meaningful degree of success may very well make welfare look like a step up and feel like a place they deserve or are supposed to have. Some have less to work with at birth. There are those who are lazy and pursue disability as life's employment, but those who think that way exist in all races and income levels. The wealthy can camouflage their numbers by picking up the slack of underperforming family members. The middle class can downplay their numbers by stating the blame as an economic slowdown or a short turn in the road. The poor has no way to conceal more poverty when a downturn or calamity hits.

A mindset must move from limited thinker to possibility thinker. If it has reached the limit and the light is out, igniting a spark to get the fire burning is not possible. An individual, family, or community engrossed in failure, poverty, and bankrupt and malnourished by an unfertile ground cannot and will not produce what is foreign to its makeup. It reproduces itself.

Who stands to gain the most by ensuring that this truth in inequity remains the same and that candor is shielded from those who need it the most? There is no reason why we cannot plant a more fertile ground.

Justice

Justice is not something inside us that automatically springs up naturally and takes up space alongside eating and sleeping to dwell in each of us forever. Justice must be fought for forever!

Loyalties

Loyalties aligned along racial, national, tribal, religious, social, political, or any other grouping with disregard to the pursuit of the truth is a conditional loyalty of limited value. If the agenda is continuously changing along with competing interests and when the stakes get higher and higher, it becomes more difficult to determine if support is genuine or strategically calculated. The nastiness of such activities becomes par for the course. How you play the game is not even a consideration when all that counts are winners or losers. When conscientious decisions and right or wrong become secondary to loyalty, as far as this subject is concerned, there is no higher calling than allegiance. If obedience is always the final answer, it is not likely the best ideas will flow to the top.

Master Plan

I do not blame the poor for being poor. I blame the rich for poverty. I do blame the poor for participating in the perpetuation and commiseration of poverty. Robbing, drugging, fighting, killing, raping, and maiming needy individuals like themselves mean they are engaging, maintaining, and ignoring the pitfalls that exacerbate an already-stressful situation.

The poor are either unaware of the cause and effect of their behavior or they don't care. There is the belief that this mentality was sown by the rich. Either way, that practice, not changed, promotes and sustains generational poverty. Its action maintains and promotes a bankrupt state of mind.

In the beginning, God created the heavens and earth. In the start of the American experience, those who invoked God, saying, "All men are created equal" diverted God's plan immediately for their own by referring to some men as masters and others as slaves. It's the genesis and genius of where the rich created poverty. A man equal in the eyes of God is not allowed to share equally in the value of his work. He is not allowed any portion of his work. Where does the wealth of his work go?

The master man's mind is permitted to expand through education, creativity, and the free pursuit of its highest potential, while the slave man's mind is forced to linger and decay, supported by laws that made it illegal to pursue even a little education. The channel to comprehend and figure out one's poverty state is blocked by the one who created it. Those of the master's kind who took no part in making decisions about the creation of poverty but benefited from those decisions share some blame because of their silence.

The slave was made to depend on the master for all things. By forming a no-benefit, no-voice worker's class, the master was able to extract all the wealth and benefit from this group for generations. It created generational poverty while reaping maximum wealth and profit for themselves. It was not in the master's interest or plan to help the slave move beyond his current state. To do so would have forced the master to do a thankless but necessary job known as work (labor). It would have opened the market to competition from a class that was better at doing that job than him. Had the slave been given the opportunity to acquire the learnable management side of labor, the master might have ended up working for the slave in some capacity as some of the master's offsprings are doing today.

Over four hundred years later, the forces that created wealth and poverty are using different and advanced tactics, but they are still producing the same results. Sustained poverty is no more of an accident than sustained wealth. In a world of random occurrences, it is mathematically impossible to have a run of such repeated good luck, while another group has the exact opposite run of bad luck without a manipulation of forces from a favored team to a favorable group or a direction by some entity in behalf of a favored group.

If the wealthy needs poverty to be maintained at a certain level to create wealth, the law and media are tools to leverage to get it done. Welfare programs are not established by the poor. To qualify for the programs, one must fall within or below a specific poverty line that is known, created, and managed by the wealthy. Even the management jobs that are better-paying jobs within the welfare programs are not held by the poor. They are assigned to the lower wealthy class to serve the interest of the more important wealthy class. The wealthy seek to privatize any and all government and poverty programs, not to help the poor but to cipher money from the poverty entitlements into private corporations all while blaming the poor for its failure.

The poor are sometimes mistreated for seeking assistance from programs set aside for them. Many trying to escape welfare are penalized beyond what they can afford. The wealthy needs the numbers to remain within a specific range to capitalize and promote the message that the poor are lazy, do not want to work, and indeed, don't want to get off welfare. The ways and means to get out of debt are shaped by the wealthy to encourage and enable poverty. It creates a pathway to dependency and not independence. The wealthy class is mingling in the higher education system in a manner that increases profit for them while pushing college students closer to poverty.

The wealthy, by their means and ways, know what economic state the poor will occupy. The wealthy knew where the poor were going to end up before they did. The wealthy also knew that they would probably be angry, mostly uneducated, and that they would put them against one another in an endless fight for nothing because real wealth and power are not theirs to have. The wealthy will label them bums and thugs while pretending they care by saying they are creating jobs that the poor won't take. They know very well many are taking two or three poverty-wage jobs but still can't get out of poverty.

Labor is a necessary and significant cost of doing business. The master knows that. In the beginning, the plan was to pay nothing for work. Private prisons are just another form of reinstituted slavery, where the wealthy get to capitalize on the use of free labor again by legal means. They get to benefit from the poor's frustration and irresponsible poverty-induced behavior.

When slavery ended, it was such a blow to the wealthy that they were willing to fight or, at least, use their wealth to convince the poorer of their kind to fight and die for their cause. After many deaths and a loss by the wealthy class, the wealthy were forced to come up with a minimum wage that shaped generational poverty. A minimum wage was a step up from slavery and another variation in the history of the creation of poverty. When disputes arose, the agreed-upon figures were either reduced or denied because in the end, there was nothing the poverty class could do about it. There have always been strategic tactics set by the wealthy to ensure that an individual number of workers are available.

As time passed, the poor class started demanding that the wealthy do more; the wealthy class balked, citing economic reasons. Finally, they sought a new exploitable labor market for undocumented immigrants. Later, it was the foreign sweatshop markets where they could amass even more wealth by paying workers without rights and regulations two or three dollars per hour. The wealthy has ciphered enough money now that they can dismiss the poverty class altogether by replacing them with robots. How to rid poverty has never been more than a dressed-up lip service from the wealthy.

In the US, they may have had to pay fifteen or twenty dollars per hour. Not only did the master create poverty in the United States, but he has also built debt all around the world by continuing to export the same poverty-wage strategies he used in the beginning, all while saying the rich care because they create jobs. Creating jobs is a business matter that often has nothing to do with caring. Whatever the wealthy can legally get away with to increase the bottom line is their goal. Another generation of working poor that the wealthy will again label as lazy is when they are no longer willing to work just to get poorer. Slaves who no longer wanted to work for nothing were lazy or shiftless. It is the wealthy-class gentlemen's tactic that has become a trademark to portraying themselves as the good guys while dismissing the working class. The wealthy will persist in feigning ignorance on the creation of poverty.

The wealthy could have done a better job in the distribution of wealth and still had more than enough wealth to be okay. Greed has never been and never will be one of a human being's best qualities. Both groups will always be dissatisfied.

The capitalistic system is the most significant economic system of our times. It is not perfect. Accepting and adjusting to criticism, especially that associated with greed, have been poorly mishandled. The state of the poor is the most explicit evidence of that failure.

Poverty is not just a by-product of the wealthy class's behavior; it is their best and most consistent creation.

Mastermind

A mastermind is a highly intelligent person, principle, or plan. Masterminds direct a problematic or complicated project or task. Napoleon Hill lists mastermind as his number 2 principle in *Keys to Success: The 17 Principles of Personal Achievement.* I am going to extend its utility beyond business or specific projects to life in general.

Most mental development is not in a vacuum. Rarely does a mind operate alone. Great executive decisions are best with the consultation of a group of other minds. Everyone has a mastermind group whether they acknowledge it or not. Some mastermind groups are formerly arranged and may have intentional and definite goals. Most mastermind groups are organized unintentionally and have indefinite goals and severe consequences. Monitor who and where individuals consult and bounce their ideas off, and you can predict with some degree of accuracy what kinds of outcomes are forthcoming.

On some level, masterminds evolve from environment, culture, and upbringing. People tend to latch onto who or whatever is handy, often without fully knowing the intent, consequence, or outcome of that association. Sometimes results are not until months or years later. Occasionally, people reject specific mastermind influences or select opposing masterminds to prove they are grown and can do it their way.

Parents and family members are part of almost every initial mastermind alliance. Depending on the sustenance value derived from that arrangement, it may result in a very important springboard or an unfortunate sinkhole. Children born to drug-addicted parents, as their first mastermind alliance, must dig themselves out of a hole. Sometimes it has to be done within the environment that helped put them there.

When I think about my family, I reflect on what my parents were trying to give to its members. I ponder, assess, and rate outcomes based on the level of acceptance or rejection according to each family member. The principle of wealth building was not in my parent's toolbox, but the policy of successful living as a person was. When my sibling and I were young, rebellion and resistance seemed standard for the course. That was not inconsistent with the youth of today. The hardness of each family member determined whether my parents' mastermind principles got through.

Using the analogy of a hole and level ground, comparing families and youth development on a continuum, if the family mastermind alliance left you on the flat ground, you are much better off than starting out in a hole. The truth is, many times, when it comes to children and their parents, a certain level of rebellion by children is confirmation that the generational gap is at play.

In a recent conversation with my niece Khadijah, I was trying to access her mastermind group when I asked about her life and with whom she was spending time. She balked, as many do at a certain level of questioning. I took it as an invasion of her private space. I have heard comments such as, "My parents want to run my life and just don't want me to have any fun" or "My parents act as if they have never done anything wrong." Such comments and activities that support those comments would diminish the effect of the first mastermind alliance even if it were an excellent one.

Napoleon Hill talked about Henry Ford's mastermind alliance with Harvey Firestone, Luther Burbank, John Burroughs, and others and how the combined mind power propelled him from poverty and illiteracy to one of the wealthiest and most successful men in the world. It is true that two or more minds working in harmony toward a single purpose have a much higher chance of achieving success than one mind. An unfortunate truth also is that throughout history, there are countless scenarios where two or more minds joined together, knowingly and unknowingly, are more successful at failure.

One case that brought this home to me occurred when I was working as a program assistant for the North Carolina Department of Correction. Seven or eight guys committed to a low-level drug operation in Moore County gathered and discussed how a particular detective was responsible for harassing their activities to the point they needed to do something about him. Reportedly, as they drank alcohol and smoked cannabis, one idea was to off him. Seven or eight minds gathered in a mastermind arrangement, but not one mind thought that idea needed more thought or thought it was a bad idea. They collected what they believed was necessary to get the job done. There were so many minds and bodies gathered that all could not fit in the passenger area of the car. Allegedly, two got in the trunk, and one had to stay back. When they reached the detective's house in Hoke County, one rang the doorbell, and another opened fire with a shotgun, killing the detective and injuring his wife. All received prison time, including the ones in the trunk and the one who stayed behind.

Unfortunately, this is how many of our masterminds are working today. The multiplication of ignorance and stupidity is highly successful in accomplishing grand follies. A genius gathered singularly or frequently, ignorant of what constitutes success but aligned on a trajectory counter to success, will hit its mark every time. To complain of where it hits without an honest examination of why it crashed keeps the mastermind on track to repeated failure.

What is significant about the mastermind principle is it yields the same multiplied power, knowingly or unknowingly, when duly organized. The effort to achieve requires the same amount of energy. The natural consequence of an unfortunate or ill-advised mastermind group can culminate in a lifetime of misguided achievements.

The Money: Listen or Hear the Government but Follow the Money

How are we being represented by our government? Or is it, who is our government representing? Am I paying enough attention, or am I paying enough to get enough attention? What about "for the people and by the people"? Isn't that applicable to the American government and its entire people?

At the time of this writing, Wikipedia listed less than two hundred countries in the world and three primary forms of government—capitalism, socialism, and communism—with numerous variations within each type. Many states practice two or more kinds of government. For example, the USA is not entirely capitalistic because of how it provides some services for its citizens.

In the history of the world, there have been numerous government structures; all were set up to dictate, rule, manage, or facilitate its people, its systems, and its properties. Often, governments intentionally favored one group much more than another, even when the message states otherwise.

As I watched the different media networks argue positions, I asked, "Is there more than the one United States?" As elected officials represent their constituents, representation along party lines seems to be more important than any other line. What is lost by almost all elected officials, regardless of their political affiliation, is the ability to represent the United States of America. When it comes to our alleged unbiased media, one must continually guard against the message, the messenger, and the spin on the message. Sometimes I do channel flipping just to get a balance of all the viewpoints. Mostly I get unbalanced. It's like a game of mental dodgeball that can be a bit overwhelming at times. When my friend Paula asked me why I changed channels, since I already knew what they were going to say, I almost agreed until I remembered I had been surprised a few times. "You know the networks established positions," she said.

I replied, "I have an idea, but I can't say 100 percent until I take the time to listen."

There is a difference between hearing and listening. The more I thought about that exchange, it dawned on me that many people, like my friend, probably hear messages. They listen, convinced of the angle, and then formulate conclusions based on preconceived notions. It never dawn on them that their judgment is only a reinforcement of their internal narrative. They are also probably utterly oblivious to how such preconceived mental framing or barrier blocks, defines, and limits open-mindedness. When making a case as a good listener, it hurts creditability.

When I was a school counselor, I had a routine exercise I conducted with students to simplify the difference between listening and hearing. In this activity, I would have students turn their backs while other students would make different noises by knocking things over or whispering different phrases. Then I would ask the students with their backs turned what they heard. Nearly 100 percent of the time, the students would give different answers. Now I had a student knock one thing down or whisper one statement, but when I questioned the students about what they thought the noise was, I got many different responses. Rarely would a student ask for clarification as if it was an act of shame. For my clarity, I would ask the students if they had a hearing impairment or any other neurological issues that would affect their hearing. When I would get a no from everyone, I would explain how this little exercise was designed to clarify the difference between listening and hearing.

Hearing involves sound or noise, and everyone heard the sound or noise even though they could not make out what the sound or noise was. Listening requires understanding, so sometimes one must listen more than once or more intensely to get a better understanding. To accomplish that task and to get the full benefit, one must engage more than their ears, i.e., hearing senses. So when a teacher tells you that you are not listening and you respond that you heard her, your response to hearing her is true, but it confirms you were not listening. The teacher wants you to engage all your senses: hearing, sight, touch, smell, and taste. All these need to be activated to get the full effect of what it means to listen.

When people are passionate about something, they become one with that something. I would say to my students, "I want you to become passionate about listening." You know, like you are about your little boyfriends and girlfriends. When it comes to your little friends, you do not miss much. When your friends are not listening and you know it, you won't tolerate it. You put them on blast, or you put them in check. You demand they fully engage with you. So you already understand the concept of what your teachers and I want. Active listening promotes learning.

I thought that this little exercise was only useful for my middle-school students. I didn't expect it to apply to our educated voters and media pundits. However, the more I thought about it, the more I believed the middle-school students are more astute at learning and understanding the difference between listening and hearing than politicians.

Politicians appear to be too busy concentrating on making their points or making sure their spins stay as close to the party line as possible. Listening requires an actual evaluation of input, which has little to do with party lines. Maybe the students just didn't have the intellectual aerobics to feign like the professional politicians.

After watching both presidential candidates' messages, I learned each group had few kind words to say about the other. Both claimed to speak the truth. I wondered if it was authentic or just scripted. One group was hearing that government was overused or overdepended on. The other team understood government was too intrusive and needed to downsize. I was a little confused because our political system is a governmental system. Both major parties were raising and spending gobs of money, using leadership PACs (political action committee), super PACs, independent or corporate PACs, labor donors, and lobbyists to influence that despised entity—the government—to its side.

Beyond all the hoopla and misinformation, what comes to mind for me is, follow the money, and you must pay to play. Why is there an argument pitting the lower and middle class against the upper class when practically everyone making the cases are benefactors of the high level?

Nearly all the candidates and officeholders of our federal government are from the upper class. I have yet to hear one story about how a top-class entitlement from the government officials will be scaled back to appease a lower level or common class. I do not think the lower class has lobbyists. Aren't the lobbyists trying to get a benefit from the government for the ones who hire them? Are lower-class taxpayers excluded from paying for those benefits? Is it any different from the advantages the poor get from the government that the higher class complains about paying? I am not trying to advocate for the correctness of either, but I am asking for an equal comparison. Did I miss something? Is it a maneuver to get me not to follow the money? Using lobbyists as financial strategists is not much different from using bankruptcy as a business tactic. An upper-class economic exclusion or set-aside is a benefit. The lower economic class may scurry for benefits the upper level would not be caught dead trying to get. It all amounts to real money from the government coffers.

There is nothing ingenious or original about high-class stealing. Stealing is stealing whether you are doing it with a three-piece suit, well-pressed shirt and tie, or with your pants hanging off your rump.

I must admit that in an age where everyone seems to be pushing transparency, these disclosure rules that allow suspension of filing reports to who knows when are making it difficult to follow the money. All parties utilize or, shall I say, take advantage of disclosure rules. Sometimes it is the rules that allow independent donors to list themselves as an LLC. Other controls enable corporate donors to donate through a nonprofit where only the name of the nonprofit organization is registered.

What class has the power to devise rules to keep one from following the money? Why is there such an effort to scurry to hide the money? Who derives the benefit if I keep track of the money? Who wins if I cannot follow the money? A lot of effort goes into individuals and groups researching the best fit for their money. I hoped the US Supreme Court did not conclude that donations are made to exercise a political right without regard to motive. If so, it is delusional.

Megadonors have grander schemes and agendas and are not modest about following their money. In this pay-to-play world, they often know what federally funded project, initiative, or policy change their cash is influencing before they donate. If double-crossed, as sometimes occurs, because of a candidate, let's say a member of Congress, overcommits or oversells and cannot deliver, then we may as well call him/her a former congressman. If he/she performs, some of the proceeds from the projects, initiative, or policy change will be ferried back into the congressman's coffer either for his/her commitment or a later project.

There have been instances where corporate donations to an individual judge's political campaign have become suspect due to favorable rulings in cases against that corporation. What group will fight to get a cap on interest rates on short-term loans, payday loans, or credit-card loans? Who will they most likely support, and what will they most likely need the policymakers to do for them? Will a stranger be able to answer that question just by reviewing the transcripts of a political conference or fundraiser, or could he/she get a clearer picture only by following the money?

This pay-to-play environment creates proportionately more opportunities for one class versus another when the government's action facilitates a development, a project, or an initiative that spurs ownership and management employees for one class and laborer employment for another class. A by-product of the multiplication of this process over time creates class discrepancy, sometimes referred to as a permanent underclass. Because there is only one pie, there is just so much of it to go around, so as one group grasps a benefit, if it threatens the interest of another team, then it's "Oh well" to that team. Do not put that dump in my backyard. The opposing group may not live there but may stand to make a lot of money for it being there, and a lesser team may not have the political muscle to stop it. Who can pay enough to put it there or who can pay enough to keep it out becomes a part of the political jostling where the only thing both parties are listening to is money. It is unbelievable that one group claims the other is using the government to fulfill its agenda and vice versa.

It is as hypocritical as trying to get me to believe that if I follow the money, I will end up in Kansas, or perhaps Dracula really is following the bloodmobile to conduct a blood quality-control test. The disinformation from all the factions is enough to keep a CIA senior operative baffled.

In summary, I think both major political groups are counting on no one listening. Beneath the claim of bashing each other for using the government, both maintain a standing invitation and open-door policy to the government. One can tell just by following the money. Money is neither conservative nor liberal; just follow it.

Microcosm

I think of America as one family. As one of nearly two hundred families/nations in the world, America is believed to be one of the richest. What is two of the most important things a rich family may provide its members? The best health care and the best education come to mind. A wealthy family will have no problem making this available to its members. Countries around the world with less wealth are doing it.

Why is that a bother to some Americans with money to burn? Why are some who have the best health care and education for themselves and their family okay with other American family members having no education or health care? Where is our "we are all one family" thinking on this? Some family members are unworthy of being recognized as a part of the American family even though they live and pay taxes in America. The best health care and best education should be available to all because of our prosperity.

If this were reversed in a way that the wealthiest American family members were denied access to the best health care and education, I think it would be addressed. How do we justify providing for some members while denying others? Poverty-stricken families are given a pass for not providing the best education and health care to its members because their resources are used to provide food, clothing, and shelter. In a wealthy family/nation, it is inexcusable. Until we see other children as ours and not "those children," we will continue to view one another as separate. We will treat those "others" differently. Those "others" may as well be foreigners until they are needed to fight for America. We are okay with those "others" fighting and dying for our American family in wars.

We are all a part of the American family. Our wealth is spent or wasted on many things far less important than health care and education. Every member should grow up knowing he or she will get the best education and health care available if we can afford to do it. It should come with an encouragement to participate in and help uplift and strengthen others to be the best they can become through a chosen profession. This is the duty and expectation of a wealthy or blessed family. Our American family spends a lot of money uplifting other families/ countries around the world, and indeed, it should if we can afford it. But to ignore and neglect its family members at home is a tragedy.

It is a household problem reminiscent of America's founding principle to leave the women, Indians, and African Americans behind. Education was thought to be wasted on slaves. As a developing, struggling, and less prosperous country, we were able to pay for some of the best education for some of our American children in foreign countries, such as England, France, and Spain. This foreign-education practice benefited America. It was a good thing. It did not go far enough to include those American families left behind.

When a wealthy family chooses not to provide the best education and best health care to all its members, it is a poor choice and bad investment. By not investing in its most valuable resources, it is placing an unnecessary burden on its preferred members, and everyone loses. When all members are not afforded the choice to pursue and become contributing members, they will become dependent members. A country or family that can afford to facilitate the longevity, independence, and productivity of each family member is investing in its longevity, independence, and productivity. To witness our welfare and disability rolls grow and not see the lack of investment on the front end on health care and education as the greatest contributory lack is not only shortsighted but stupid. There is enough potential knowledge, gifts, and talents rotting in our prisons and group homes to probably save not only America but also humanity. Our choice not to cultivate every resource from birth to death means we must settle for what was cultivated. Our nation/family is falling behind in education and health care. The current trend is grossly inadequate and unsustainable. If we wish to continue to be one of the wealthiest countries on the planet, investing in the health and education of one another is indispensable. It is not welfare. A country that is unhealthy and uneducated cannot long take care of itself and will soon need the assistance and care of a healthier and more educated family/nation.

The Real Conservative Principle

There is a lot of conversation about conservative principles versus liberal principles, that is, if liberals have any beliefs, at least according to the conservatives. It is fascinating to me to see how different sides line up to promote their agenda as if there is a lot of difference. A true liberal or a real conservative tends to view his or her truth as "no other truth, so help me God."

A conservative believes one should conserve the use of resources in the assistance of others to not undermine the resourcefulness of others. If one is in trouble, the most likely cause is himself. Therefore, get himself out. Resources that were most likely created by those less wasteful and more responsible should not be available. It only encourages more mindlessness. It also reduces the available resources for everyone. If death is the outcome, that's collateral damage. It is a worthwhile price to pay to slow the proliferation of stupid behavior.

In the final analysis, resources are not entitlements and are not unlimited. To take our limited resources and give to someone who is most likely responsible for depleted resources imposes an ill-conceived partnership on all. To those who choose to live in the most liberal and laissez-faire fashion, let them accept the full costs or consequences associated with that "anything goes" approach when things go wrong. Every man should pay his way and pay the piper if this is his choice. "I should not have to subsidize man-made misfortune," says the conservative.

I can agree with a great deal of those positions, including the last one. However, oversimplification comes with some blind spots. Not all misfortune is self-induced. It is not always easy to isolate the origin of disaster or to diagnose the perpetrators due to the size of our country and the intricacies of setbacks. It is not easy or simple to separate the contributors to the resources from the manipulators of the resources.

We all live in a society that was set up for the benefit of everyone. At least that was the idea behind "every man is created equal, with certain inalienable rights that among them is the pursuit of happiness." Not everyone had a voice in how this was to work, so those who did not have a seat at the table had to trust that their interests were debated thoroughly and pushed forward with the same zest as those who were at the table.

Some misfortune was sown even before the meeting of the minds at the table of inception. Early conservatives were conserving resources for themselves and their interests. Those funds compounded interest over the years and produced even more resources. Those accumulated resources were not entirely self-made but self-manipulated. The deciders in the distribution of wealth at the top had more leftover at each paycheck to reinvest, while those contributors to wealth at the bottom were unable to meet weekly obligations. They were forced to borrow at a higher interest rate from those invested funds they help create. The wealth gap grows wider when the production distribution over time amounts to a disinheritance for some and the greatest inheritance for others. And guess what? It was legal. The conservative claim that people are wholly responsible for their misfortunate due to failed liberal ideology. It is a grossly irresponsible assertion. Conservatives who promote such claims are perpetuating misfortune as just outcome. That conservative-assisted misfortunate is a current mainstay.

Material misfortune is measurable; however, the mental and cultural argument are much more massive and devastating. It contributes to a mindset of devaluation and disillusion that is generational and too widespread to ameliorate with social programs, which only abate surface misfortune and assure continued adversity. One must qualify to receive consideration for social programs; therefore, one must maintain a position of hardship or poverty to receive benefits. It is a fake-out move by the conservative to argue and pretend they are against these programs, so the needy think it is a prize and fight to maintain the misfortunate status, while they continue to amass more fortune with good old-fashioned conservative deception, sorry, I meant, conservative principles.

The expanding of resources is that same conservative trickery to widen the gate to trap more misfortunate to get and rely on crumbs. While the liberals are occupied, arguing, and demanding more freebies, the real conservatives are going after the bigger fish with the knowledge that more impoverished are isolated out the market of the actual moneymaking game.

The buildup of enough favored distribution of production/wealth affords political access, which eventually allows exclusions and favors. It facilitates fortunes for some and accelerates misfortunes for others. A better word for this style of conservatism is privileged.

When one sees corporate and elite favors as entitlements, permissible, and deserving yet sees preferences for a lower class as despicable, it smells of hypocrisy or, shall I say, misfortunate created unequally. The suggestion to redistributed corporate favors and entitlements would be viewed as liberal folly.

Some people have things done for them; others have things done to them. They thrive; the others faltered. One can embrace what he gets. Another must find a way to move forward from what he got. There are those who call the shots; and then there are those who keep taking the shots.

In society, everyone is expected to contribute according to one's capacity; all are to benefit as a community is able. Those wishing or used to carving out a piece of the rock for themselves to the exclusion and at the expense of everyone else, whether conservatives or liberals, are neither conservatives nor liberals. They are high-tech hustlers and swindlers in the same old game with a modern spin, still making a fortune without any competition in sight from the misfortunate. Conservatives ascribe to a self-enriching distribution of wealth that they know will contribute to an increasing number of impoverished who will line up for more goodies of which they will argue vehemently against. Now, is that a liberal idea, or is it just conservatism at its best?

Chapter 7

Racial Lines

African-American Journey

This article pertains to the African Americans' journey to and within America. It is not a slight to the struggles of any other culture or group in America. It does not claim to be so factual that every statement is unchallengeable. It is the author's opinion and understanding of accounts. From 1555 to 1865, the passage from bondage to citizenship was prolonged and difficult. African Americans have traveled through the halls of Congress to the presidency, in and out of the statehouses, and back and forth to the supreme court. With every earned success, there has been blood, sweat, tears, broken bodies, repeals, and setbacks, all designed to eliminate or severely weaken gains.

Through it all, African Americans have demonstrated allegiances to this country by fighting and dying alongside their captives in the American Revolutionary War to help gain freedom from Britain, knowing that freedom would elude them at home. In the Civil War, World Wars I and II, and all the US wars afterward, African Americans have shown their solidarity against all foreign and domestic threats to freedom, again, knowing it would not make much difference to their liberties at home.

What other citizens have fought consistently for over four hundred years only to hang in their uniform for seeking lodging or a sandwich that had to be purchased and consumed at the back-door. African Americans along with their fellow soldiers have been spit upon for participating in an unpopular Vietnam War. African Americans got treated as second-class citizens, while Germany's prisoners of war got honor and respect.

As late as 1963, a person of Asian descent, who recently arrived from China, would be allowed to ride alongside a white person in the front of a bus, while a tired old fourth-generation African-American lady would be arrested for sitting in the front of the bus, even if the seat was empty.

During 1789 to 1803, twelve amendments got submitted for ratification. African Americans had lived and worked in America for over two hundred years by then but were three-fifths of a person and considered property. None of the amendments applied to them. Property did not have rights.

Everything about the African Americans' journey has been designed to make and keep them second-class citizens. African Americans and Europeans came over on the same ship. Usually, the passengers chauffeured are famous people. They were not chauffeured. African Americans were not passengers; they were cargo. Because they were live cargo, they had to be chained and kept in bondage. This baggage might do more than shift during travel. Deaths of this baggage, not through fault of the slave but due to improper storage and handling by the owners, were discarded like common garbage by being dumped overboard. Trips from the African coast to America could take as long as two to four months.

It is difficult to imagine how Europeans could portray themselves as upstanding citizens and southern gentlemen, all while raping and abusing their property, especially women and children. This property was kidnapped, stolen, or purchased through shady dealings with African warlords or tribe leaders. Some property was exchanged for spices and other overinflated merchandise.

The African Americans' journey is unimaginable, unbelievable, and in many cases, untold. The African American stands today as a witness and a survivor. The European mission and intent were to take the survivors, break them down to nothing, transform them into a permanent labor force, work them until they are useless, and make them suspend all thoughts and pursuits of happiness in the present. The plan was to mold them to expect joy, peace, and happiness only after this life, all while they collected the fruits of their labor in this life. The Europeans did not create this afterlife; they just modified and perfected it for their purpose. God was said to be a chartered member of the White Citizens' Council. Induced and targeted ignorance is a designed plan to keep African Americans down and marginalized.

Niceties are deceptions. The spices and sugars of yesterday that African Americans chose on the shores of Africa that started this journey are the same false goodies used with the welfare and social programs of today that bind and blind African Americans from their real purpose, worth, and strength. Killing and selling one another out in their communities as they did on the shores of Africa unfortunately also continues today. It is the best evidence of how successful the Europeans have been in stripping African Americans of their worth and value despite the lengthy and arduous struggle for justice. It also confirms the journey long sustained is far from over.

Black-on-Black Crime

Black-on-black crime is not an insult or slight to the legitimacy of similar concerns with other races. Crime against nature or the planet is a significant concern. Let me try to simplify black-on-black crime without slipping in the mud of semantics.

For once, I do not want to use a lot of statistics; we have too many slanted or designed to foster agendas. I do not want to argue. We do too much of that with meaningless outcomes.

I read an article recently that concluded there was no such thing as black-on-black crime. It stated, from 1976 to 2005, African Americans committed 94 percent of African-American murders. During that same period, 86 percent of whites made all the white killings. So crime was a wash. Proximity and opportunity were to blame. We had that same space, locale, and chance to eat one another but passed. Sorry, that was a slip into semantics. I did agree with the portion of the article that said crime is not black or white.

What is at the core of the killing, robbing, raping, or assaulting that occurs more often in the black community by blacks predominately to the population? Why is responsibility often attributed to our history or nature as people, nation, media, system, parents, lousy community, rap culture, schools, or guns? I understand contributing factors such as poverty, disenchantment, and marginalization, but not as deciding factors.

I heard a story once about a man doing cartwheels in a bar where he was warned before he slipped, fell, and was injured. He sued the bar owner for his accident and blamed the establishment for his wounds.

The neighborhood, family, or country that helped in our development is not perfect. Our history as a nation is shameful as well as magnificent. It is our history, and it is unchangeable. What we can change is the present so that our future, which will become our most recent history, will be more magnificent and less shameful.

I may be a little off the mark. It seems rather simple to me that if one finds himself in a house taking property and belongings he did not purchase and he enters by kicking in the door, his country, family, and neighborhood are still whatever they are and where they are. He is in the house, acting alone. If a crime is being committed that requires real-time presence and involvement and I am not there, I certainly do not want anyone blaming me, even if it is my child. Going down the road of declaring if he had a better school, finer parents, superior upbringing, tremendous opportunity, or terrific society, one is dismissing the reality at hand and is off on speculation or conjecture. Even if all that were true, the current truth is where we are and what we have before us. The more we deal in what-ifs, the further we get away from "what is."

I am concluding this story with a conversation I had with an inmate when I was working at Hoke Correctional Institution in Raeford, North Carolina. The inmate was going on and on about how young people have no respect for one another and are killing one another when I just had to stop him and remind him of why he was in prison. He stated to me that his case was different and that the man he killed had it coming. "The man had already shot a couple of people," he said. "I could not take the chance that he may have been more successful with me." In other words, he did society a favor and perhaps saved two or three more lives in the process. How many of us, like this inmate, think we are heroes in black-on-black crime? It is time we take a serious look at the man in the mirror. We do not need any more heroes. Black-on-black crime merely is a cultural log in our own eye.

Diversity?

I wish I were capable of comprehending and absorbing the available knowledge within our universe. It would produce a level of diversity that would make me very unusual. I am okay with that. There is so much unknown that a lifetime is not nearly enough time to find. Diversity is the recognition that all knowledge is limited, incomplete, and forever receding in completeness due to the speed at which the universe unfolds versus the rate at which human consumption is possible. Because there is news occurring simultaneously all over world, and that is just one planet, information left unknown and uncovered has continuously grown for centuries, so what we know is too pitiful for anyone to pronounce himself as knowledgeable.

There are thirteen major natural regions of the world defined mainly by latitudes and hemispheres. Most conversations I have ever been privy to hinge on mostly Western, sometimes Eastern, and on rare occasion, Far East knowledge. That does not cover the whole world. So I will concentrate on my very limited diversity, the West, and that is limited even further by what the US news outlets consider newsworthy.

Acquired and retained knowledge comes from universities and scientific, media, social, and other outlets. It makes up a large part of a diverse population of ideas and thoughts that are constantly infused with historic, generational, and current information. Recent accounts of fake news, conspiracy theories, and disinformation have made their way into the mainstream. Although available experience is vast and varied, the nature and reality of daily individual consumption and travel restrict and restrain functional expertise to a specific region. So Westerners and Easterners would most likely be more knowledgeable of their territory.

Within Western and Eastern cultures, we find different thoughts, beliefs, and customs among the many different areas that make up the East and West. In the Americas, the diversity from North, Central, and South America is vast and distinct. The various areas of the United States produce differences and similarities.

Individuals advocate according to their exposure, which is limited by whatever particular stage of human growth a person has obtained at the time. We cannot speak intelligently about things we have yet to learn. There are those who will speak on what they do not know as if they do.

We are casually aware of the vast body of knowledge within our universe and our lack of intimate daily interaction with it, but we rarely talk about how much of it we do not know.

Knowledge obtained from a region is essentially confirmed and reconfirmed by familiar members. Years of confirmation by everyday and familiar individuals only serve to consolidate and constrict one another's positions as being knowledgeable. Limited disagreement means nothing if we are just protecting our friendships and family alliances.

A more in-depth look into these regional positions of knowledge posing as global wisdom explain the difficulty in changing or invalidating an opinion shared by a region or group. So as it spills into politics, philosophy, or religion, the cry is the same: "I am wiser than you because I was learning when you were in diapers." And that is proof of more age, but it may or may not prove more knowledge.

When the knowledge acquired from a region is contrary to the understanding of a different region, the yeses will outnumber the nos when the one doing the counting is from the same region. To honestly check regional arguments posing as global sophistication takes independent arbitrators. It is to the point we need to get opinions from a different planet.

When it comes to politics and religion, we yield nothing. It is why it is a universal rule in some places to never discuss these subjects. It is also why little growth occurs in these areas.

We refer to North Korea as a closed society. Aren't all nations closed to a degree? Maybe North Korea is more closed based on the criteria being used to measure openness. A more significant problem is the number of closed minds.

Unlimited freedom may produce a more diverse learning environment, but it will not produce a complete knowledge. In a virtually untapped universe, there are potentially solar systems of knowledge that will forever remain unknown. The immense diversity of the universe makes Easterners and Westerners kinfolks.

My Spirit: A Treasure or a Tragedy

I am questioned when I say my spirit led me to ask this or that. Great thoughts are not pushed forward without internal grappling. They are quite different from knee-jerk ideas. There are documents of humanity wrestling with the meaning of life and God. Because of the spirit that dwelled in man, there is probably a longer list of undocumented accounts of many thoughts of unknown people like me who push their mind down instead of out because of fear of retribution. Breaking from religious, cultural, and national worldview is often unpopular, unwise, insane, or genius. I wondered if we, as a society, have been robbed of our most significant ideas due to the institutional power structure's discouragement over the years. The authors of what's right are called instigators or agitators. People of goodwill and honor have stood silently in the face of ignorance when wealth and power were aligned against them and portrayed as right.

Slavery and the Jim Crow era are perfect examples of ignorance ruling, as a potential wealth of knowledge was forced to lie dormant within the minds of many African Americans, Indian Americans, females, and even some Europeans. Currently, there are countries maintaining traditions of ignorance that trump the spirit of many great minds by disallowing them to be educated, to drive, or to participate to the best of their ability. Culture, academic, and religious constraints are often economically bound and aligned opposite critical thinking. There are those in our society who believe that our Civil War produced the wrong winners and that things would be better had the south won. The intelligence of the time knew that slavery was wrong and that slavery did not advance the betterment of humankind. Shortsightedness and ignorance colluded and became suitable traits that promoted economics and community standing. A segment of society with equal biological and natural characteristics institutionally sees itself as separate and superior to another part. This ignorance is a choice masquerading as intelligence. If the preferred segment woke up the next day as a member of the inferior group, a reversal of behavior would ensue. All proponents of slavery will become opponents if they awake the following day as slaves. The nature of God is better understood by the superior class when slavery, an unnatural fit, is unleashed on him; even his intelligence grows.

Racism Is the Base

There is a lot of talk about political parties playing to their base. The deception is, the bottom represents a marginal part of the group, but they do not control the much broader and more inclusive ideology. I intend to debunk this double-talk and tiptoeing rhetoric as nonsense. The base and the more massive party are all the same. The more significant and less vocal part is content to play ignorant, and let them say what they do not have the guts to say. Those who have little have less to lose and more to gain in the way of a return to the good old days—the days when just being a certain race meant something. Those with more have more to lose, so there are advantages for them to be quiet. They are exposed if paired with evil racial ideology in a society where all races matter. They are sophisticated enough to know that those days are gone forever and that there are economic prices to pay for missteps. They know we must contend with one another while benefiting from feeding their base the big lie that a return to the good old days is around the corner. They are pitting the poor against the poor and stressing that European Americans, the original framers of the country, should matter more than anyone else. They are emphasizing that European Americans are losing their place on the mantel at the top and are being asked to share and stand beside others. Somehow yielding to an equal standing is accepting a lesser American. That is not what the framers intended. Had they wanted it that way, they would have included everyone at the table from the beginning. Knowledge of "what was" and "what is" is now at odds. It is what keeps this nation bottled up in never addressing the elephant in the room.

Let us go back to the founding of the country. Every president to Lincoln needed to address slavery. By ignoring the right thing, with rationales flowered with splendid and sophisticated English, year after year, they just kept kicking the can down the road. Administration after administration chose not to act while declaring themselves as courageous patriots to the American cause of freedom for all. The base saw the early leaders as bold; they made brave stands for the only interest that mattered, that of the European Americans, unlike the Chicken Little leaders of today.

You see, slavery was never an American cause. It indeed was not worth standing up for against the interest of European Americans, even if it was morally right. Americans would rather pretend the slavery issue was not an American issue but an African-American issue. In fact, as the early leaders were kicking the can down the road and standing up for American values, it never mattered to them that other costs existed among theirs that were just as American as the ones they held. African Americans fought and died alongside European Americans. They were not given full credit as Americans. Many Americans fought for the causes and values of America that were neither European American nor African American. There are many statues all over this country today that signify who were the great early Americans who represented the heritage of this country. The great first African Americans either were not a part of the American culture or were not Americans because rarely a statue exists.

Although European Americans' history overly represented one race and overlooked other races as the norm, they did not see themselves as racist or believed their actions were racist. The base honors every early slaveholder and credits them with being more American than other Americans. Many do not believe they are racist or their ideology is racist. They believe this country has lost its honor and toughness. It is too soft. Its leaders are passive, not ruthless and rugged enough to run roughshod over everyone as Andrew Jackson did with the Trail of Tears. A few broken-down slaves never stopped old Rough Rider from being great. Such heritage is blue-blooded, patriotic Americans carrying out God's will.

The base's belief today of who is American and who is not American is in line with this early European-American thinking. If the support is not the majority, then the majority must answer the question of where it stands by not only denouncing but also acting with those who condemn regardless of the party affiliation.

There are always many other factors to consider, but who is American is the first matter of interest when attacked by others. Therefore, it must be the same when assaulted by others. In a country built and promoted as freedom and justice for all, there is nothing more American than coming down on the right side of the race question for all Americans.

I heard it said that Americans were victims of Britain. Slavery was an inheritance from England that was forced on them to make payment to the English crown. America did not disinherit itself from slavery after it freed itself from the British monarch. In all its effort to be different—a "shining light on the hill," a "beacon of hope and freedom for all"—it failed to yield to the right thing the interests and values of the least among them. America did not see a need to leave slavery behind. Slavery and racism were at the base of the American experiment. To say that racism represents the fringes of America and that it is evident by a small and marginal support, so little that it was able to elect a president, is nonsense. It makes no sense to attach to a small group with whom you have no agreements, especially one not large enough to matter, unless by claiming the large group is small. It serves the big picture of your values and interests. To gather with any group of racists while propping one up as a moral leader is as hypocritical as a hungry cat chasing a mouse, insisting it is just playing.

John C. Calhoun, a prominent senator from South Carolina, called slavery a "positive good," and a "peculiar institution." Calhoun was a staunch proponent of slavery. History portrays him as an eloquent speaker and a statesman. He is a tremendous southern hero. He represented a way of life that is still honorable and respectable today in certain circles. No apologies offered, and none is expected or forthcoming. The African-American race of people was inferior to him in every way, incapable of receiving full citizenship, and useful only as a laborer. Their function for life was to contribute to the permanent elevation of the European-American race. From Mr. Calhoun's perspective, it was a perfect fit; and to this day, some of his cheerleaders still hold those views and conduct their lives yearning for a return to 1840. A more extensive group within his race is content to let the narrative play out and take the benefit without ever going on record. That position is in line with Edmund Burke's saying: "The only thing necessary for the triumph of evil is for good people to do nothing."

As the spokesperson for many who could not find the words to explain the dilemma, Calhoun's position of authority provided a rational narrative. He created a platform that normalized division and painted those who opposed slavery as agitators and more responsible for evil than the slaveholders. With justification in hand, the European Americans had what it needed to carry out Jim Crow law. It provided for separatism laws to flourish as right and just, while antislavery laws consistently got the shaft. Many who held opposing views sat around and watched this go on year after year took the gains and remained quiet. These armchair racists did not vanish or evaporate into thin air; they multiplied. Their children's children are a part of today's American landscape. They never left. Many are making their voice heard as the base. They adamantly deny any racist's history, only heritage. Who would ever think of considering Andrew Jackson a racist? He was a great American, a patriot! Today many proud patriots line themselves with a political party and stand shoulder to shoulder for an American cause that includes only European Americans. Those fringe groups who declare themselves as racists are at least honest about who they are and what they want. If the truth is known, if things could revert to the way they used to be, it would suit that party line fine.

When some hear racism paired with them, they often change the subject and call that distancing themselves from those people. They are continuing to vote with them. They enjoy the benefits of being a part of the ruling party. Those who despised the way things used to be but benefit from the advantages of sticking with the ruling party need to tell the truth and get off the fence.

Signs stating, For Whites Only or Go to the Back of the Bus were never thought of as European-American problems even though they always were. It was never the job of the African Americans to sit at the lunch counters or to get rid of signs saying, For Whites Only. European Americans initiated and instituted it; therefore, it was a European-American-created problem and theirs to solve. Imagine me creating a problem, pretending to have nothing to do with it, and telling you it is your problem to solve. By creating and establishing it, one should not back away from owning it. European Americans, the original creators and framers of policies, are also responsible for creating the conditions and scenarios within its borders that allowed and caused racism to root and flourish.

I have heard it said, "This is not who we are; we are better than this." No, this is exactly who we are. We are great and dignified people; we are also shameful and misinformed people.

Our democracy has racism baked into it. Many of European descent who stood idle or participated in sitting at the front of the bus, using bathrooms for whites only, and eating at lunch counters that said Whites Only were enabling, benefiting, and encouraging a wrong, knowingly or unknowingly.

Tribalism Uncovered

There is this thing called tribalism on my mind lately. It is not new, but its use in the last few years has heightened. Many free and independent thinkers perhaps disagree and think a tribal trend doesn't sway them. Unbeknownst, we are firmly in the grip of tribalism as I speak. Our first tribe is our family. We do not get to choose that tribe, and when given a choice, we often choose family. From elementary school to college and beyond, we join clubs and organizations in a tribal fashion. Tribal living has mostly served us well against foreign and domestic dangers and threats since the advent of time. Tribalism is not a bad ideal or practice. It is practiced badly, or it can become a bad practice.

Jesus said, "Follow me; I will make you fishers of men." From this statement, one universal question as our guide should be, "Is the leader worthy of following?" Is he willing to lead by example? I can see how children become victims of poor tribal leadership by parents, but can someone help me understand the willingness of adults to follow poor leaders?

Every cult or extremist movement since the beginning of time possessed elements of disqualified leaders or failed agendas from the outset. Mindless participants glossed over the presence of flawed tribalism in Jim Jones's Peoples Temple and David Koresh's Branch Davidians. It is replayed so often in history that it should alarm casual onlookers. The rise of Adolf Hitler's Third Reich and other state or tribal government creations have left enough human destruction for all humanity to be clear on the tribal issue by now. Following without questioning means missteps abound and persist. It makes me wonder if humankind is truly the highest cerebral functioning species. We tend to throw our support according to history, family, country, custom, tradition, party line, or popularity with a total disregard for truth and honesty. It is shameful, but more importantly, it is dangerous.

As a school counselor, it always amazed me when parents were unable to distinguish support from enabling. Stating "In this family, we support one another without balancing it with the facts of a situation" troubled me. Vindicating a child based on his last name and without a full review of the facts was the norm. "Blood is thicker than water" is what I heard a lot. It was more like ignorance is thicker than evidence. Upholding a child in wrongdoing is not support; it is simply wrong. It sets him up for future conflict beyond a parent's control. There is no inducement to pursue what is right when just being a part of the family or group makes it right. There is no need to be the best person one can be, just the best member one can be. One is rewarded for loyalty and penalized for honesty.

When dishonesty becomes the norm for a tribe that is in a position of leadership, those who are not a part of the tribe are displaced or subject to harm. They lose their sense of value and purpose. They don't feel they will be treated fairly without towing the tribal line. Compromising or conceding is not a part of the tribal dialogue. It inevitably spurns the growth of more tribes to combat tribalism.

We have the Never-Trumpers or the Forever-Trumpers. It sounds like the Ride and Die slogans of neighborhood gangs. Tribalism is rooted in a superiority thinking that puts itself above examination. It is either you are with us or against us.

News outlets such as MSN and Fox present tribal ideology wrapped up in a news format that is making millions of dollars. One problem is, they are exceptionally good at what they do. A continuous supply will reinforce a tribal slant one way or the other. The effect is thought to be marginal. It is another misstep. Not thinking or realizing something is a problem while being under the influence of that problem is the definition of a major problem.

As an observer traveling throughout the south, I notice televisions on the Fox News channel all day long as if no other channel is worthy of watching. This subtle conditioning amounts to gradual hypnosis that is responsible for creating a chorus of enablers and cult-like followers. Those who supported slavery as a norm without actually holding slaves were enablers. Germans who went along with relieving Jews of their property and placing them in concentration camps without taking them to concentration camps were enablers. Blind loyalty is just blindness and ignorance. It has proved destructive for centuries. It is just as devastating today. Decency no longer exists. "I could stand in the middle of Fifth Avenue and shoot somebody, and I wouldn't lose any voters. They let you do it. You can do anything. Grab 'em by the pussy." These statements would be a problem if said by a third grader on the playground, yet under these tribal rules, it is no big deal. The bigger problem is not that it was said but that the person who said it was telling the truth. It is comparable to the sad truth that everything Adolf Hitler did was legal. When one is allowed to get away with wrongdoings, there is no reason to stop doing wrong. I don't believe everything is about race, but for this tribal leader, I believe there is a sizeable racial component to his survival in spite of the many reprehensible things he has said and done without reprisal. And I can prove my racial accusation with one statement: let him wake up tomorrow morning black. Supporters would scramble for a way to distance themselves from his tribe without sounding racist. Even the black tribal supporters who hate their own race would leave him. This tribal leader would probably tweet, "Out of here." Sobering to admit, but this tribe operates under a cloak of secret racism.

Too Much Appeasing

As someone born in the south and lived my entirety, I have acquired a peculiar cultural and custom skill set of understanding that may be misdiagnosed by someone who hails from a different region of the country. A term like *southern gentlemen*, I have heard all my life. Too often, it has been conflated with irreproachable older statesmen, able to deny constitutional principles and equal rights when it conflicted with the interests of the Negro class.

Of the fifty-six signers of the declaration of independence, only thirteen did not own slaves. The first Supreme Court chief justice, John Jay, owned slaves. Appeasement is more formerly recognized as compromising and negotiating. The impact of these negotiations is shameful and incredulous. The founding fathers erred badly when it came to ensuring the part of the constitution that referred to "all men are created equal." The founding fathers and their collaborators were loath in admitting it as a mistake. History has produced plenty appeasers, all portraying it mostly as a minor hiccup, while creating narratives of themselves as oversized characters with impeccable character, as in the case of George Washington's "I cannot tell a lie."

The whitewashing of the term *slavery* in such language as "persons held to service or labor," "peculiar institution," "domestic institution," and "conditions of servitude" are part of a continuous pattern to dignify slavery with flowery words in a time when three-fifths of a person is recognized as factual and covered by the law. It is hard to get eviler than believing one has the right to purchase a person for two or three hundred dollars and then think one owns that person and anything conceived and born of that person from now until eternity, even in the case of owner's molestation and rape. To top this evilness off, the slaveholder believes he should never be relieved of this lifetime ownership right without just compensation, but no compensation is ever just for the slave or his descendants for eternity. That ideal of democracy would be stunningly unbelievable if it was barroom gossip, except it is true for a country that portrays itself, according to Ronald Reagan, as "a shining city upon a hill whose beacon light guides freedom-loving people everywhere."

Time and time again, constitutional delegates agreed that a strengthened union of the states was more important than the revolutionary ideal of equality. From the Washington's administration to the Lincoln's, the can was kicked down the road, leaving the answers to the slavery question to each succeeding administration.

Failure to address slavery fully and truthfully fostered the spread of racial inequity into new territories. The Missouri Compromise of 1850, the Kansas-Nebraska Act of 1854, and even the Dred Scott Supreme Court decision of 1857 were compromises or bargains to appease the confederates' way of life.

The Buchanan's presidential administration facilitated the Corwin Amendment, which would have, in effect, dissolved Congress of any power to interfere with slavery in the slaveholding states. It was another last-ditch effort to appease after seven states had already succeeded before the start of the Civil War.

Northerners who attended the West Point Military Academy with the confederate soldiers and fought alongside one another in the Mexican-American War found themselves pitted against one another in the Civil War that was made inevitable by the founders' lack of foresight and appeasement. Although some confederates may have given up a few acres of land, no territories or states were lost as is normally the case in war. Had the south won, I do not think the southern gentlemen would have been as nice and forgiving with their terms. They most likely would have forced slavery on the entire nation. I am almost certain no statue of Ulysses S. Grant or any other union soldier would have been erected. The United States of America may have become the Confederates States of America. Southern states got to keep all its states and enact black codes law, which allow them, in many cases, to re-enslave blacks. After a minor glitch called Reconstruction ended in 1877, another compromise was handed to the southern states with the installment of the nineteenth president, Rutherford B. Hayes. He allowed many things to return to the Pre-Reconstruction era. The losers in the Civil War were granted an agreement that effected the removal of federal troops from the confederate territory. They enacted a Jim Crow era of legal racial discrimination with another appeasement courtesy of the 1896 US Supreme Court decision in the Plessy v. Ferguson case of "separate but equal." They erected statues of their losing warriors all over the country in honor of who knows. Why is there an amazement of what would happen without penalties and structures?

Part of honored burden depicts the dishonor of those called to serve and their failure to step up to the plate to institute dishonorable discharges to the instigators and to enact the withdrawal of lawful privileges to the confederate states while restoring "all men are created equal" to the union. It should have been a no-brainer condition of surrender. Instead, the victors acquiesced to more appeasements.

The inability to acknowledge that fighting one another had anything to do with slavery was mostly another appeasement to save face for the south. The north was not blameless in this one, because after all, both camps colluded in profits. Who wants to admit and accept the blame for the fighting and killing of over 750,000 neighbors and family members over that three-fifth property thing?

The American experiment started sometime before the Jamestown settlement in 1607 with a few indentured servants. A few indentured servants turned into millions of "persons held to service or labor" and an economic boom that propelled the rise of a nation. It cascaded through the Revolutionary War and the Civil War, along with centuries of appeasements and multiple southern gentlemen's arrangements better known as popular sovereignty agreements.

It is now 2020. There is talk of a second civil war. When will we learn there never was a gentlemen's agreement to be made with southern tyrants? Arthur Neville Chamberlain's appeasement of Germany's tyrant, Adolf Hitler, in the Second World War provides us with the best understanding to what happens when you appease a tyrant. Those who made the choice to side with the Confederate States of America against the United States of America were all tyrants, traitors, and treasonous. Today's national problem is rooted in placating the southern confederates far too long without a scalding condemnation and retribution in lieu of admiration, glorification, and appeasement. Take it from this southern gentleman. Dismiss with the damn appeasing, please.

Chapter 8

---❦---

Innocent Bias?

Air, Please

O ccasionally, thoughts run through my mind about the genuineness of people in position to make decisions about helping people they know little about due to the casualness of how they go about making decisions. Sometimes they make decisions designed to help the lives of others with no knowledge and little desire to learn about the living condition and circumstance in which they reside. Decision makers usually acquired these roles through political, academic, or monetary means. Now, of course, this is rarely thought of as a problem because it is the norm. They generally prefer to rely on information from bosses, friends, or associates they trust or information that is read or reported in reputable circles or media forums. They are usually too big, too important, or too busy to go out in the field and get firsthand information.

When I heard Sen. Bernie Sanders say the system is rigged, I cannot help but ask, "Is this supposed to be a news flash? Why have you been bashing in it for so many years without telling us?" It is evident to me that those we look to solve our problem are part of the problem because most do not have firsthand knowledge of the problems. How can a Donald Trump tell you he is going to fix your problem when he has never known your problem? As a self-professed lifetime winner, he has lived his entire life making sure he never had your problem. In fact, he believes if you have such issues, they were self-created as his success is.

When our founding fathers were not willing to include women, Native Americans, African Americans, or any other minority ranks at the table for the first constitutional delegation, fixing the problems of this new country did not include settling the issues of the excluded members. To do that properly would have required their input. When a group concludes they know what is best for a separate team, it is from their knowledge and in service of their interest. It is not an oversight. It is an "undersight" and an intentional act. To tackle the problems of others is to suspend one's issues long enough to examine other people's problems.

Those in power on both sides of the aisle tend to look out for themselves and a select group of friends while claiming to be looking out for the middle class. They are not a part of the middle or lower class, therefore, could never be fully invested in those concerns.

All interests are not equal. Some interests get real access to power. Lobbyists help ensure specific interests are addressed time and time again, while other benefits get lip service. If, as a group, you are unable to affect a person in power, your complaints or interests are of little interest to those wheeling power. Because it is the right thing to do, never sway one in power who believes the power holder should determine what's right. For it to be correct, it must be in line with serving the interest of whoever is in power.

The rich and powerful people help those in power stay in power. Those in power make sure they stay rich and powerful. Now and then, these two groups will throw the poor and power-less a bone just to make them think they care about their interests. In a wealthy country, lots of money is available for many interests. When the same groups are helped over and over, it is not an accident. How is it that one segment gets addressed all the time but always needs help? It is exactly as Mary Trump says, "It is too much and never enough." Yes, Senator Sanders, the fix is on, but it is not news or new.

I Am Not Alone…in What I Think I Am

Our births are creations of God. No other entity is a creator of life. God created man as a human being before and above everything else. Humankind is a product of a natural act. As we came onto the scene, millions of other creatures of God were already on the scene and a part of a perpetual phenomenon. Unbeknownst to us, there are ecosystems and insects and other animal systems already in place, working very well together before man's intervention.

Instead of man blending in with nature, man set out to dominate and redefine nature. Definitions of man's institutions of mankind will eventually take the place of God's or nature's intent. It assists in facilitating the best economical use of human beings and every other species. It is essential that everything and everyone fit nicely in some compartments, such as Native American, black, white, republican, democrat, American, Italian, Christian, Muslim, and so on. If none of these categories work for you, then there are others, including antisocial, misfit, thug, gangbanger, Blood, Crip, skinhead, and many more.

Throughout our life, without revisiting the Creator's plan for us, we pursued harmony with the world mostly through accomplishment within one, two, or more of man's categories. When is the last time you received praises, money, or award for being a great human?

Most eventually align with something or become an outcast, which is just another man-made slot. Our identity and status depend on fitting in somewhere. The mastery and accomplishment of these categories can be profitable. Respectful existences as republicans, black men, Christians, thugs, skinheads, or Muslims all can bear fruit. There is a likelihood that harmony with God will never gain its rightful place.

Individuals conclude that whoever they are best known as is what they are. The height of what we ascribe to be and become is the level of accomplishment within a category. Society's rating of that specific group will add favor or disfavor to the individual standing within a community or on the world stage. Lost in the fray, again, is God's definition of who we are.

A case in point, a whole man is born. It should have been hard to reconcile even four hundred years ago how a man could conclude that a black man was three-fifths of a man after God had determined him a full human. Man's institutions went along with it and redefined the black man for economic purposes. It facilitated the creation of a peculiar institution called slavery. The fact that it conflicted with God's creation of all humanity alike mattered little. Accepting such an institutional definition of humankind over God's definition over four hundred years ago is like the actions of institutions today that seek to redefine what God or nature intended. Naturally, there is no difference between a republican, democrat, Christian, Muslim, Buddhist, Blood, Mexican Mafia, thug, skinhead, and any of society's categories.

Society or institution titles seek to elevate or oppress, depending on who stands to gain or lose. It has absolutely nothing to do with truth or the true nature of God's creation. To the world, it will carry the most weight. There are those who still say slavery was fate or God's will or intention. Historical inaccuracies abound, and man's justifications are rampant: God intended for the Arian race to rule the earth. Whites are biologically superior to blacks, and we got the science to prove it. We are unequally yoked; therefore, God endorses unequal treatment. You and I, at our base and core existence, are products of God. Everything else is a product of man's making or imagination. To turn a blind eye and deaf ear to nature's facts denies God's accomplishment in the genius of you. Accepting three-fifths as a whole man diminishes that man and subjects God to the will and whim of man. God is no respecter of man.

Identity Crisis

The clash of identities is present and real, not only in this country but also around the world. I am going to concentrate mainly on what I understand or see going on in the United States.

The battle of identities is more along economic lines than any other demographic. It is a class struggle. There are mainly two classes: upper and lower—the haves and the have-nots. Middle class is only a euphemism. The upper class uses messaging to confuse others into believing there is only a slight difference, and with a little hard work, it can be made up. No one wants to acknowledge or identify with the lower class. One way to opt out is by identifying by other metrics, such as race, skin color, status, and even uppity attitude.

Let me explain how identity crisis works, at least in my mind. The upper class is where most desire to be even if the lower level is critical of the upper class. Most pursue and prefer an advantage over fairness. Sen. Bernie Sanders's recent talk about a rigged system is not unfounded. The rigging is to secure a better position in all dealings.

Affirmative action programs' design and intent are not to reverse unfairness in place already. It is not to take away anyone's job. Affirmative action programs are not new. Jobs have been provided to one group by policy for years. It was not seen as affirmative or discriminatory because it was illegal; it was the norm, an upper-class privilege. The same set-asides of the upper class are railing against with poverty entitlement programs. Skin color and privilege, for some, are the same. If one is born with it, indeed, one should not be penalized; however, one does not come by skin color and privilege the same way. One is natural, and one is man-made. I concede that innate differences should not affect policies.

When things have been a certain way for an exceptionally long time, it can have the appearance of occurring naturally. It is not uncommon to acquire a sense of entitlement that seems logical. If I have a great job, lots of money, and all the more beautiful things in life, I believe I have those things because of my great-great-great-grandfather who legally owned people who worked for free. I am sorry. I had no hand in any of it. It was all legal. Why should a person be relieved of anything or penalized for anything that was legally acquired? It is purported that everything Hitler did was legal. Should it never be rectified?

A law that governs years of living that grants preferential treatments and positions for one group and disadvantages to the other segment, with the disadvantaged having no input and no recourse as normal, is an unjust law. What is the remedy? It is the first and most potent affirmative action. The playing field is not just slanted but also wiped clean; others need not apply.

A status quo with significant benefits does not evaporate on its free will or because those receiving the benefits complain they are unfair, old, and boring. The benefactors of the superior positions have the power to do something about it. They also have the most to lose. Why cut off the hand that feeds me? If the shoe were on the other foot, would I be as content? The class that is the product of the most significant affirmative action is also in denial. The law opened the doors of opportunities for one group for centuries but slammed the door shut and locked it for centuries to another. It was not affirmative action; it was an action affirmed.

It brings me back to my original point. People say all they want is justice and fairness. The problems lie in people's interpretations of what is just and fair. Just and equitableness always mean an upper hand to one group and pretense of the same thing for another. Even the US Supreme court once ruled that separate but equal was fair.

It is not that the superior group is unaware of inequality; the upper class has been active in strengthening its position for years and may honestly, by now, believe they have earned everything they got.

This article rests on economics. The race argument is a diversion. It depends on how it benefits the bottom line of the upper class.

When it comes to justice and fairness, even a stalemate is a win for the person with the better hand. It means nothing changes. It confirms that justice and fairness must wait to a later time. Justice is delayed, and injustice is continued.

Identity is a crisis. Superiority thinking is entrenched. It has more motive to remain the same than giving an inch.

Justice and fairness are subordinate constructs to economics. Slavery attested and confirmed that. The identity crisis for the lower class is a construct of the upper class.

Reality

When I hear people use the word *reality*, they tend to express it as if it is an absolute. Well, for some describing reality, it may be as factual as he or she has lived and experienced. Because others probably have had different experiences, even when some of the lessons are from some of the same people, places, and things, their existence may still be different. I think the values we place on our reality become too personal to be objective. Others who are challenging our understanding of reality ruffle egos. Arguments become a battle. If arrogance emerges, the facts or merits get lost.

I think we all have cultural and racial components of reality that blend with environmental and geographical elements, which are weighed differently from individual to individual. The outcome for one person with a similar fact can be different, so other variances appear when we factor in differences in era, race, culture, and other significant unknowns. When people are arguing about the superiority of different upbringing and backgrounds and attempting to highlight the merits of one reality while mocking the existence of another, it stands to reason that butted heads dig in, concede nothing, and learn nothing.

I agreed to purchase a house from a person who happens to be Caucasian who quoted me a specific interest rate. He assured me I would receive a certain interest rate if I got my financing from "his" bank. I entered the agreement with his assurance. When I attempted to explain how it might be different for me, he insisted that he knew many of the officials at the bank personally and doubly assured me I would not have any problems. Later, I shared with him a different figure that was given to me. When I told him who gave it to me, he was utterly blown away and said I was mistaken. The people he knew would never be involved in anything but complete fairness in their dealings. He was speaking honestly from his reality and knew nothing about my experiences even though we existed in the same community and era and dealt with the same person. When he confronted the bank official on my behalf and explained he had promised me the same interest rates quoted to him, he was told he was quoted a military discount that was unavailable to me. I do not know if he bought that explanation, but amazingly I predicted a contraction before there was a contradiction.

My reality, though different from his, did not have any illusions. His acceptance of the explanation may lead him to believe that all discrepancies, in fact, are just misunderstanding and that my presumption, which turned out to be reversible, is just me being hypersensitive, suspicious, or paranoid. The banker's explanation and willingness to change and give me that rate may have convinced him that his friends were still as honest and fair as ever. It may never dawn on him that I would have never got that reversal without his intervention. It is a privilege that is a norm for him and one I do not know.

That is often the story of most realities and why the "realness" of experiences, in many cases, is only real to the individual and serves to insulate us from one another. It is nearly impossible to admit truths of which we have no experience, even if we live among them daily. It is the reality in plain sight that we all miss.

When a person is right about his or her reality, the argument is less about the merits of right or wrong and more about an honest review of both positions and their traditional strengths and weaknesses as well as their contributions and contradictions. Positions or successes cannot be validated exclusively on one's reality. No one should ever conclude that accomplishments are the sole result of race, family, political ties, or geography. They are factors, but there are intangibles weighed differently by similar and dissimilar realities. When a reality surmises that the absence or lessening of barriers is insignificant, then reality is stuck on stupid.

The Struggle Continues

When the Europeans arrived in America, escaping from religious persecution and lack of freedom, they set their sights on becoming successful on this new continent. Democracy and freedom were the new buzzwords for the government of the future, with a twist. They would persecute and deny liberty to minorities and women. Oh, and they would enslave one group.

The democracy is established to favor some and provide disadvantages to others. It was a democracy with favorites or, depending on who was speaking, democracy with a congenital disability.

Education was illegal for some yet promoted and facilitated for others. So what was behind the move to not allow this great benefit to all groups? The group making that decision perceived a more significant benefit for themselves. They also expected to receive a collateral benefit from the group not to be educated.

In a caste system, expectations are very slim to none of moving beyond the economic group of birth. This democratic system was not a caste system, but it had its similarities. An uneducated class was more useful as a labor force. This group would only need to do as told without questioning; the more unintelligent, the better.

A religion that reinforced total obedience tied to a God who sanctioned one class over another class came in handy. The superior level could not take a chance on allowing a religion with equal standing to give a junior class any ideas of challenging total and complete submission. Freedom of religion meant not only believing in the superior group's religion but also facing retribution for not. Freedom of speech also needed to be checked at the door. Offending the power structure or superior class is forbidden and, in some cases, unlawful.

The inferior class had to understand that everything told to them or done to them was for their benefit. Behaving in a doubting or disbelieving manner was unacceptable and often run afoul of the law. If it were not unlawful, it was treated as a customs violation until a law could be passed to cover it. Religious verses were cited to make all this rationale.

As for that other group, Native Americans, who occupied the land and appeared slow in conforming, the introduction of alcohol, diseases, and sex succeeded in deluding and tricking them out of much of their health and land. What not acquired or manipulated by reneging on treaties was overturned or voided by new laws that favored the superior class.

History notes this as just another example of excellent European intelligence at work over a lesser intelligent form of life. Illegal actions were made legal. Reviewing authorities declared there were no rights of inferiors that superiors were obligated to obey. The superior class thought and believed, "What sense does it make to set up a country and then give away rights and privileges of equal value to a person one feel is inferior in every way?"

The struggle continues in the face of certain beliefs. The first African-American president Barack Obama's legitimacy was questioned continuously and undermined by a culture of superiority thinking within both houses of Congress. Time has passed without growth on the original thinking on who is superior. The ruling authority's position is unchanged. The belief is, they belong to a superior class ordained by none other than God himself.

Walk This Way

One of my favorite early adulthood hangouts in Southern Pines, North Carolina, was a basketball-court area known merely as the Clay Hole. Do not ask me why they called it the Clay Hole because I have seen many mudholes or areas where there was a lot of clay that did not have clay anywhere in their names. So I guess someone called it that, and it stuck. I lived about four blocks from it for nearly twenty years and never heard it called anything else, except when it was shortened and just called the Clay.

One late afternoon of balling turned into a game of hide-and-seek. The darker it got, the more jumpers were missing their mark. Passes were hitting players in the head. It became apparent the darkness was trying to tell me it was time to call it quits. Guys were gathering their boom boxes, collecting their keys and afro combs, and making their way out of the Clay Hole. I was a little late in preparing to leave when I noticed I was having trouble finding my keys. When I held my head up and looked around, all my buddies had gone. For the life of me, I could not believe a set of keys got away from me that fast. After about ten minutes of futility, I was getting frustrated and angry, mostly at myself for letting darkness catch me and allowing everyone to leave. Now this was pre-cell phone days, so I could not call anyone. Just when I was getting tired of using those four-letter words on myself, down the road came a perfect specimen for me to get out of my frustration. It was the town drunk, taking one step backward and two to the side. I thought to myself, *This drunken guy best not stop here. That is, if he ever gets here with the way he is moving. The way I am feeling, if he slows down here, I might go off on him.* I said, "The last thing I need now is this wobbly joker questioning me while I am trying to locate my keys." He did finally make it to where I was, but he was stumbling and drooling. I thought, *What can he possibly do to help me?* Before I could say something to him, he had the nerve to ask me if he could help. It took everything inside me not to curse him out. I paused and said, "I do not think so." I wanted to tell him that he could help me by keeping it moving, popping a clutch, continuing to stumble down the road, and, oh yeah, watching out for the ditches. I decided to humor him a little by answering his questions. I said to myself, *He cannot even find his way out the middle of the road, and he is going to see my keys.* So I told him I lost my keys somewhere in this grass, and I was looking for them. I guess he thought he said something ingenious when he said, "Maybe they are in your car."

I wanted to say, "I have already looked there, you drunk. Now if you are all out of bright ideas, why don't you make like a frog and hop on down the road?" Instead, I said, "They have got to be out here somewhere in this grass because I always take them out of the car for extra security." I wanted to add, "In case some sneak drunkard thief like yourself decides to jump in and take a joyride." At least out here, he would not know which car the keys belonged.

Since he wasn't going to go away on his own, I thought I was going to either have to give him some wine money or just be plain rude to him and let him know that he is useless. Instead, I decided to play along with him and grant him his ridiculous request by showing him that my keys were not in my car. I walked over to the car, and he stumbled behind me. I opened the car door and searched the console, the dashboard, and in between the seats. He said, "Maybe they fell on the floorboard as you were taking them out, and you thought you took them out."

I was thinking, *This guy is beginning to get under my skin, and I am getting tired of being Mr. Nice Guy.* I said, "This drunk is worrisome." I wondered if I could get away with just throwing him in the ditch. My blood was beginning to boil. I was moments away from unleashing a barrage of four-letter words when my hand felt some keys on the floorboard almost directly beneath the ignition. Now I had been to this car twice, looking for my keys, and here was this drunk, making out like a prophet guiding me exactly where my keys were, all while explaining how they most likely got there. All my buddies left me, yet he was the one who patiently stayed with me until my ordeal was over. I was so stunned and outdone that I was speechless. When I offered him a ride and some money, he turned them down and said he did not have far to go.

I had seen him staggering around town many times, but this was the first time I ever had a conversation with him. I had no idea he was that sharp. I thanked him, and we went our separate ways. That chance encounter taught me a new appreciation for him and all the others with similar situations. That part of his story has made it into my account as an inspirational piece about listening to everyone regardless of the walk of life.

If you dismiss people without hearing them out because of who you think they are or because of who you think you are, you may miss something significant. Also, there is no exclusiveness on genius. Even a fool may say something inconsistent with his norm. That old saying that even a stopped clock is right twice a day may be appropriate here. Besides, you never know who God may use to send you a message.

Let me end with this if I may: What happened at the Clay was not something for which I would pray. It was to my dismay. But because he walked this way, declaring that with me was where he would stay, he dispelled my fray and allowed me to say, "Amid the confusion of an afternoon of play arose an unlikely hero to save the day."

What If?

Most agree that early-childhood development is critical to success in adulthood. This is a story to test your honesty, prejudices, and biases.

What if I told you there was a guy in charge of an early-childhood education program who produced an over 97 percent success rate of college graduates? What if I told you all the graduates could speak a minimum of three languages fluently? What if I said to you that along with their high scores in academics, they were also well-versed and well-rounded in social, athletic, music, fine arts, and leadership skills?

It is the twentieth year anniversary of this program's existence. Many of the graduates are leaders in business and government around the world. This program is the recipient of countless accolades. Educators and parents across the globe attribute much of the higher-education spike to the graduates' civil commitment to volunteering a specific number of hours each year. There has never been a rumor about the honor and integrity of the program. It does not surprise anyone that there is a waiting list for parents to enroll their children. Most students who qualify for the program eventually get in or receive some tutoring.

Keeping the founder anonymous allowed leadership to focus singularly on content and outcome. Some credited its success to the anonymity. Because this program produced such remarkable and consistent results over the years, very few people cared or wondered about the founder.

New Freedom of Information Act in education recently forced a revelation about the founder and three additional what-ifs.

What if number 1: What if I told you the founder was black? Knowing all that you know about the history and success rate of the program, are you still as excited as ever about putting your child in the program?

What if number 2: What if I told you the founder was gay? How will your thoughts, views, and feelings about that affect your decision to place your child in the program?

What if number 3: What if I told you the founder is also an atheist? There has never been any hint about any of the founder's personal views interfering with program integrity. Are you having second thoughts about your child's participation?

What if I asked these questions ten years, twenty years, fifty years, or two hundred years ago? How would the level of prejudice and bias be different? What if these questions are asked ten years, twenty years, fifty years, or two hundred years into the future? Which what-if bothered you the most?

Lastly, what if I told you many of you will take your children off the waiting list and out of the program but will not be honest with yourself or your child? What if I told you your right to be prejudice and bias without honesty would do more damage to you and your loved ones than being prejudice and bias? There is nothing inhuman about contradictions; your dishonesty with yourself is proof of that.

Chapter 9

Sage Advice

Force of Habit

There is a lot of discussion about why people use force or violence on one another. Authorized force in a violent manner may be called law enforcement or may be a military strike, hopefully, as a last resort. It is deemed as an inappropriate use of force when it is used to extract gains for illegal reasons. Those improperly gained benefits are called abuses. The simple answer to why we use force, improperly or authorized, is because it works. The threat of force is sufficient sometimes. The effectiveness of this seemingly effortless choice can make this decision a habit. For those entrusted with the capacity to use power as a function of their job, it must become second nature but within controlled and legitimate constraints. Hesitation or second-guessing may result in a tactical disadvantage. Another improper use of force would be an encounter with friendlies.

I believe my father used force because it was risk-free and high reward for him. It was also readily available. He did not see the sense of value in wasting a lot of time or spending lots money just to get simple matters resolved.

I recalled, where I should have known better, when my father told me to take out the garbage, and I balked. I was feeling my oats, so I looked at him like he was crazy. Suddenly, the room went dark. I found myself crawling out from under the table. He was standing over me with a crazed look, saying he ought to stomp me. The next time he said "take," I was in his face, saying what and where. So his hard-hands approach resulted in quick resolutions and paid dividends for future interactions. It was efficient, swift, and inexpensive. Matter resolved, and case closed. That was probably the simple truth on why it was his favorite choice.

Now force does not always have to be abusive or violent, but those two layers seem to hover beneath the surface, just in case a breakdown in compliance requires it.

Now there are side effects to this type of medicine just as there are with other medications. In the situation with my father, his choice got the results he wanted. But at what cost? For the rest of that day and maybe for the next couple of weeks, it put a strain on our relationship where I did not interact with him as positively as I usually would have. I internalized some anger and bitterness that probably adversely affected how I interacted with others. There were potentially long-range damaging, hidden, or biological variables that no one could account for entirely. Adverse effects of my development could very well extend residues into the next generation. It is the reason force, as a way of getting things done, is not recommended. Abused children tend to abuse their children. Some children will get more poison from such interactions. Others receive lessons that are beneficial. It may be years later before the effects are revealed.

Force and even the threat of force can become a necessary force of habit. If law enforcement did not carry weapons, with the permission to use, some aspects of society indeed would not comply just because of their presence. There are some who would get in line because of the uniform, the badge, or the role of the institution. There is that percentage who must be cracked in the head or at least feel it was an imminent possibility before they comply.

Countries use force or the threat of force when diplomacy breaks down. Diplomacy breaks down sometimes because a nation signals force is off the table.

A pecking order of strength is often determined by who can exert the most force and who is capable and willing to use it. My long years in behavior modification and mediation training differ from my father's application of force. My early-childhood upbringing has shaped some of my views on the appropriate use of force. If my father said he was going to beat me, it would be okay for me to start exercises designed to strengthen my rump. It would be all right to start crying and hollering, because only death, not mine but his, would keep him from carrying it out. He thought it was a sin to promise something and not deliver it.

I learned that for a force to be effective, it had to be swift and in the exact manner it was prescribed. I later learned that reliance on force or making it the primary tool in one's collection could also put one at a severe disadvantage. If force or the threat of a higher level of authority does not work, one may be backed into a corner and faced with a mandate to use the ultimate force—death. I think my siblings and I were never sure about this one with our father, so we just did not take any chances.

If this is a point where you are unwilling to go, you have lost the battle. It allows the person slated for the use of force to seize the upper hand and force the negotiations in his favor, especially if you are without an adequate backup plan or an ace in the hole.

Parents who choose to use force without other creditable management tools may find themselves boxed in. You cannot regroup if you do not have anything with which to regroup. All societies appear to tolerate a certain level of force to establish a balance and standard of compliance to which its people can abide and thrive. Those with the badge or uniform who choose to go beyond or outside that level of acceptability, as a force of habit, must be subject to the same authorized version of what they advocated for others.

It Is Your Word

You are all faced with situations where you give your word only to feel later there are inconveniences to execute or to fulfill a task or expectation as it relates to that word. In many cases, it is just easier to act as if it is "just a word." Maybe you can just concoct an explanation or rationalization that will satisfy your audience, at least temporarily until you can come up with something better, something outside the nagging earshot of that parent who raised you or the teacher who taught you better. Sometimes thoughts of seeing again that person you left with a falsehood lead you to places where that person is not known to frequent.

There are occasions when you give yourself a silent word, in the case of a promise to yourself. When you fail to deliver on that commitment, you tell yourself no one knows about it. When that communication is clear to you, its implication and application are no less critical than if it was spoken loudly to others. You say it is no big deal until someone does find out and questions you. Your commitment to yourself is one of eternal significance. When your word means little to others and even less to yourself as demonstrated by your action or behavior that disavows, it speaks volumes about you and to others.

Your word is an essential part of you that cannot be eradicated by more words from you, especially on the heels of words still reeling from a severely diminished state. You cannot shore up rhetoric with rationalizations and falsehoods. You shall know a man by his word.

Words are powerful, infused with all the spiritual force of humanity and creation, with such strength that one word or thought can bring a war to a civilization known for peace or peace to a society torn by war. Your word alone can move and direct people to places and decisions that can shape their day and calendar for a year or more; such callousness without regard to self and others ignores the spiritual dimension of the Word and diminishes a person's growth in the Word. Your word is with whom you start. Ducking and dodging your word announces to the world who you are and who the world is following should it choose you.

Opportunity Knocks

Life's discussions about a purposeful life from a religious and a philosophical perspective will issue different outcomes depending on a scholar's field of training. I am not a scholar of either camp.

Although the number of births is staggering, the number of failed conceptions is mind-boggling to the degree that every birth must be viewed as a miracle, primarily when the successes are against all the possibilities contained in a single ejaculation.

When my wife and I were in discussion with a fertility doctor about our pregnancy, there was a conversation about my low sperm count. It was explained that it is a ten to twenty million odds against being born in just one sex act. Every birth beats those odds. He said, "Multiply those odds by the number of sex acts around the world that never get a birth from the ten to twenty million odds, and you get a glimpse of the vastness of the miracle of birth."

I prefaced all this to create a framework for a purposeful existence beyond the religious and philosophical debate. When one wins the sperm and egg sweepstakes races for conception, then survives the rigors of possible autoimmune environmental complications en route to full term. Surely there must lay a higher purpose than becoming a bum. It is my layman's explanations why life shouldn't become mired in a shameful and pitiful trail after birth. What occurs beyond birth should be an affirmation and a continuation of a victory tour. Births are not accidental feats; they are meaningful and purposeful statements and physical representations against incredible odds.

So what is the overriding purpose of life, or what would further define our reasons for existence? If your life after birth fails to enhance the experience of others, it is doubtful your contribution with offspring would enrich or strengthen them. A life spent amassing wealth that does nothing to expand the existence of others would have been hardly missed had it never been born. A life spent mulling in gossips, put-downs, or other trivial matters mattered little to the existence of others.

Now there are many religious and philosophical explanations for life, but I wanted to lay out the layman's explanation. It amounts to an opportunity to enhance the lives of others. One must feel fulfilled to participate in the enhancement and enrichment of others. If one survived the rigors of preconception and the tribulations of postconception to birth, one has been enriched miraculously beyond what one will ever know.

Now to continue to be enriched or blessed, to put it in religious terms, you must take this opportunity called life and go out and magnify the presence of others. It is that giving back that multiplies and amplifies your purpose for birth and gives thanks for the miracle you are.

Turn the Other Cheek

Many times, when teenage boys are sitting around with too much time on their hands, kicking it about girl conquests, it is not long before something stupid is said or done. To teenagers, these ideas are often viewed as brilliant and are usually seconded by the group. I hate to admit that I recall one such incident where I was a part of the encouraging cast who got my friend Ralph in a little trouble.

It is not unusual in any era for boys to be interested in girls and girls to be interested in boys. Both spend time talking about specific body parts or what they would like to do with this or that. Restraint is taught and expected as a matter of custom and law. Giving in to dares or boosters is also not uncommon. Who hasn't, in the darkest recesses of their mind, not thought about unusually beautiful legs or shapely behinds and wondered a few too many what-ifs?

To my friend Ralph, a dare is just a harsh request that requires action. To him, a bad idea with mystique and pleasure as the outcome is brilliancy couched in an opportunity worth the trouble. Someone must be willing to take the plunge. Ralph saw it as his manly duty to act on what the group wondered. He even said as much to never accuse him of backing down from a challenge, especially where it concerns girls. I understand unbridled teenage testosterone, but as we can see in the adults misbehaving in the revelations in the #MeToo movement, some boys never grow up.

One afternoon on a routine ride home on the bus, after an exhaustive conversation about a pair of beautiful long legs, someone suggested the only obvious thing to do was to see if they felt as lovely as they looked. Requesting permission was not a part of that brilliant thought process. When five or six exceptional teenagers' minds are of the same opinion and there is no minor dissent, what is a boy to do? Comply.

Ralph surmised the worst thing that would happen to him would be a severe cursing, and who could not withstand a little tongue-lashing? He volunteered to gather the information about the texture and quality of Chenille's legs and share it with the group. Just as he began to get his rub on, like a flash of lightning, there was a pop from out of nowhere that turned his whole head around. In the nearly fifty years since that day, I do not think I have ever seen anyone slapped that hard. He had this look of "Wow!" on his face. It was at that moment that I realized maybe it was not such a brilliant idea after all. What a feeling suddenly had nothing to do with legs. Perhaps we should have spent more time discussing Chenille's firm and powerful arms or the strength and speed of her roundhouse. Showcasing teenage brilliancy in a group is always a bad idea. I learned that on that day. Too bad Ralph had to provide the knowledge.

Two Children

Every day the Lord provides us is a good day. If you do not believe it, try doing without a couple of them. I think that every day is a part of God's plan, and since God is not in the accident business, days granted are a part of God's plan and not meant to be wasted.

The story about two children is a story about choices. It is also a story about how the decision to follow the choices of others can serve as a detour that can take one off course for a day or a lifetime.

Child 1 leaves home for school full of joy and energy. She plans to make all As on her assignments and get the highest praises and smiley faces from all her teachers for exceptional behavior.

Child 2 leaves home for school also full of joy and energy. She plans to use her power in as much mischief and disruption as she can muster. She is a little tired of all the praises and smiley faces going to other people.

Child 2 bumps into child 1 twice in the hallway, and on the second time, it causes child 1 books to fall to the floor. Without acknowledging her or saying "Excuse me," child 2 proceeds as if nothing happened. Child 1 just passes it off as an accident.

Child 2 goes on to pick a fight with her in the classroom over raising her hand too high. Child 2 yells, "What's wrong with you!" The response is less than what she expected. Child 2 ups the ante and refers to child 1's mother as a garden tool.

Child 1 finally decides she has gone too far, so she says a little prayer: "Lord, forgive me. I need to give this 'thot' what she has been asking." So with all her pent-up anger, she slaps child 2 out of her chair and jumps on her and starts ripping at her face and hair as if she has gone mad. The two are separated. Child 2 is relieved that someone was present to rescue her.

Others were watching child 2's treatment of child 1. They praise her and wonder what took her so long. There is a ten-day suspension for the children.

Both children left home with specific goals. One child was able to accomplish her goals, and the other was not. Naming other people as the reason for making choices or making the decision in concert with others has nothing to do with the fact that it is still a choice. We must also accept the consequences of choices even if others are praising them.

The constant changes and challenges in an era where wrong is right and right is wrong make choices a daunting task. The more responsibility we use in exercising our options, the better we become at recognizing the possibilities that are not good for us. The wrong choices can appear necessary, or it may give us a feeling of accomplishment and joy. As for child 1, it was a life-changing moment. All the praises and accolades she received afterward started her to change her entire approach. Learning fighting skills she never knew she had, she began settling all her disputes in that manner. She replaced her goal to do well in school with an intention to run the school. After multiple suspensions, she dropped out for good in the tenth grade.

Unfortunately, years later as an adult, she was still talking about her beatdown of child 2 in elementary school as the highlight of her life. Child 2 went on to finish college and is now in a PhD program. God has granted both children the same number of days. Choices and the moments can appear insignificant, but in time, fortunes or hardships become revelations of whether God's days are wasted or used wisely.

Wealth or Riches

At first glance, they appear the same. If you placed ten dollars on a kitchen table and came back ten years later, it would still say ten dollars. The purchasing power would be substantially less than it was ten years ago. That is riches. Those who do not understand riches often lose wealth by seeking fortunes. The kitchen that is a part of the real estate, if maintained, should be worth considerably more after ten years. That is wealth.

Wealth endures and does not require constant attention and manipulation to maintain or extend its value. Wealth is soiled when traded for riches. It is lost through the endless and careless chasing of riches.

Riches have fleeing value, and wealth has sustaining value. People and relationships have a more significant benefit than wealth. True wealth accounts for relationships and seeks to enhance and strengthen relationships in the building of wealth. It is the wealth of relationships that is the real wealth for perpetuity.

What Is in a Habit?

For as long as I can remember, I have heard information about habits—most of it has been negative and have come from negative people. So what can we learn from negative people about habits that can be positive?

Throughout history, there have been some interesting quotes from an array of people, some famous and some not so memorable, about habits. Take the one from Jules Renard, "Laziness is nothing more than the habit of resting before you get tired" or "Every once in a while, someone without a single bad habit gets caught" by Kin Hubbard.

What exactly does it mean when someone says we are creatures of habit, and what is the difference if a negative person tells us that versus a positive person? As creatures of habit, is it just another habit to argue about who informs us?

In Charles Duhigg's New York Times bestseller, *The Power of Habit*, he talks about MIT (Massachusetts Institute of Technology) researchers' discovery of a neurological loop at the heart of every habit: core, routine, and reward. He goes on to say understanding your habits means identifying the components of your circles. Do we need scientists to tell us why we brush our teeth every morning before we take a shower or why we shower and then brush our teeth?

Maybe it helps to think of habits as complicated so we can dismiss the one about laziness being a habit of resting before you get tired. Or the practice of excuse making—it must be neurological. That explains why I am making excuses. There is something scientifically wrong with me; therefore, I am not to blame. And that is not an excuse; it is science.

Well, the discussion about habits is not new because in commenting on habits, Aristotle (385 BC–323 BC) said, "We are what we repeatedly do." Was he saying we are just wired to repeat certain things and, until science explains it centuries later, our fate has been tied to our habits?

For those saddled with the habit of making excuses, George Washington Carver, who also was a scientist, did not mention anything about a neurological loop. Instead, he said, "Ninety percent of failures come from people who have the habit of making excuses."

If you are one who believes you are doomed to your habits by a neurological condition and needs a complex formula or magic bullet to save you, let me leave you with a rationale from Desiderius Erasmus: "A nail is driven out by another nail, so a habit overcomes a habit".

Lastly, permit me to try to deliver you with a warning from Saint Augustine: "Habit, if not resisted, soon becomes a necessity."

Marriage or Not?

I believe I am not the only one who has wondered what is it that permits humans to maintain relatively successful relationships for a long time but get married and cannot keep it together. I have concluded that it is a mindset issue. The woman thinks, *I got him.* The man thinks, *I am got.* Although they sound similar, they are opposites.

The mindset creates different thinking as they move forward, and it ultimately dooms the relationship. From the woman's viewpoint, "I can now let up on how hard I worked to get him." She is also a little resentful and angry for what he made her do. She thinks much of it was unnecessary and in the realm of BS. If she is unable to control that internal thinking, she begins the process of getting back at him. Her weapon of choice is sex. Why? Most likely it is the same weapon she used to get him. She knows it makes a difference to him in the things that matter. Because she now has the added protection and shield of the law on her side with the marriage license, she is more reckless with her approach and action. She also thinks if he is not thoughtful, she will now be able to hit him with the second thing that matters, his wallet. Because she thinks the deck is far slanted her way, she keeps pushing the envelope.

Lastly, there is always that part of human nature that says the catch is never as enjoyable as the hunt. It is an unconscious mental operation or mindset that amounts to a slight slide in pleasure that grows with time. Combined with all the other shortsighted behaviors since marriage, doubt slips in about whether this is what she wanted. "Is this what I signed up for?" Eventually, it goes from maybe to maybe not to not.

At this point, there is no reason to work to keep it going. The growing unhappiness highlights the advantages of being single that she had long forgotten. Now that she is married and the feelings are not what she thought, she sets her sights on getting rid of him. The cycle continues throughout life. "Why I cannot know what I wanted when I got what I want?" is the question that keeps dogging her. What I wish for seems always to be out there. I am unfulfilled if I am not chased or chasing. It is a dilemma. Is it mainly because I project the blame and responsibility onto the other person?

From the man's viewpoint, he sets out to set up a pecking order that leaves no doubt that he is "the king" even if he is not bringing home the bacon. He will also go as far as quoting a Bible scripture or two to make his point. If children are a part of the blended family, they need to recognize or it will become a point of contention.

To the man, sex is now a duty, a function when and wherever he chooses. It is nonnegotiable. It indeed should never be weaponized against the king of the castle. At the first hint of reneging, he pouts and starts thinking it was all a setup and she never cared anything about him anyway. He starts resenting her and begins pulling back on the commitment. He is also starting to wonder if she is worth it. All the back-and-forth about marriage is now about who did and said what. It becomes an accusation war about a bunch of nothing that is made out to be something. Love and respect for each other get lost in the shuffle.

Neither party admits responsibility for anything. Instead of being friends beyond the breakup, it is all they can do to be friendly to each other. Somehow the love that flowed so smoothly without any pressure before marriage became love with demands, mandates, and constraints that do not flow very well from former independent thinkers.

Both partners began to believe they were duped. Both moved from "I do not think he or she is worth it" to "I do not think it [the union] is worth it." The passionate work required to make a marriage work was gone. Neither got what they thought they were going to get.

Individuals performing at an optimal level against free will is not one of society's cherished functions. Both parties' life experiences have taught them to seek additional written guarantees beyond verbal agreements. Both once enjoyed individual freedoms and loose expectations. Both attempted to invoke their freedoms while directly or indirectly asserting more demands on the other's freedom. The mindset that is developed and acquired becomes their undoing.

Although society's expectations in a marriage represent different expectations in a two-person arrangement, reconciliation to those expectations is never fully understood by either. The truth is, the relationship was always about the expectations of the two people; society's expectation should have never entered the picture as an object of major concern.

Why couples tend to get along much better before marriage than after marriage is a puzzling thing. I think the idea of marriage is never thoroughly marinated and synced with the practicality of marriage. A marriage needs deference if nothing but smooth sailing is the prevailing idea and expectation.

Chapter 10

Faith

A Leap of Faith

Stranded in what has become a hostile territory with a group of people on a religious retreat, the copilot has suffered a heart attack and is dead. You learn that your ace pilot is guilty of taking sexual liberties with an eleven-year-old who is currently on the trip with you. An investigation reveals he is a pedophile and has had sex with over a dozen minor-aged girls in the last year. There is a push by some on the trip with you to have the ace pilot banned from the group. The only other person on the journey with any pilot training is a guy who took an online course to be a pilot. He flew in a simulator once. He has never flown a plane in his life but is confident that God has created this situation just for him.

The challenge is a test of your faith in God. Your simulator pilot believes firmly that God will see everyone through and that God has chosen this very moment in history just for him, so he is admonishing everyone to be a part of history with him. Do you vote to keep your ace pilot, abstain from voting, or affirm your faith in God and stay with the simulator pilot?

It is a defining moment. A decision is needed quickly. All of you are told rebel forces will take over the port within two hours. What do you do? How do you reconcile your religious convictions with endorsing the maligned ace pilot? If everyone perishes with the simulator pilot, what is the lesson learned, and what is the message to the loved ones about your choice to go with the untested pilot? If all survive with the untested pilot, what is the word about faith? If everyone perishes with the ace pilot, what does it say about your trust in the Lord? If everyone survives with the ace pilot, what is the example for others to follow? What will you do?

A Deeper Spirituality

For centuries, many have proclaimed to be direct descendants of God, anointed ones, or perhaps modern-day saviors or prophets. Visionaries are popping up everywhere in search of a deeper spirituality. It is God's Word they must obey. They part ways from one religion and form their own. Chosen ones from their flock find disfavor and form another.

Religious disputes and splits have been going on for centuries. They have not always been amicable. I do not think we have reached a point where one can say, "It's settled, no more separations." So more searches for greater religious experiences are on the way. Sometimes these religious expansions or transitions cause more problems than they repair. Members' spiritual difference is not the only reason parishioners follow newly formed religions. Governing boards and associations of these institutions may require adherences and abdications so difficult that members move on before the new charter is signed. In search of this deeper spirituality, are we pointed in the right direction?

Economics seems to be more of a driving force behind the modern-day changes. "I don't aspire to be at the right hand of the man. I aspire to be the man." The most popular leaders and organizations usually generate the most growth and longevity. Members are more apt to talk about a popular or famous pastor as if it has real value.

A study of the history of many religions tends to depict silence on the slavery question. It is said that Jesus and Paul endorsed it and just exhorted masters to be kind to their slaves and slaves be nice to their master. Early congressmen preferred to refer to it as a peculiar institution. From what I can gather, none of those called by God heard anything about addressing that peculiar institution.

Chosen ones have promoted their arrivals as a time for a change to get serious about the Lord's business. All these changes have been to fulfill God's mission. Through it all, there have been upheavals, persecutions, and exiles but no biblical answers to the slavery question. Christ's most potent and perhaps most relevant words, in my opinion, of what he tried to teach and leave all humanity may have been, "Forgive them for they know not what they do." Today's worshippers find it reprehensible to forgive fellow parishioners sometimes for criticizing articles of clothing while stressing they are seeking a closer walk with Christ. Christ made the previous comment in response to those responsible for killing him, but somehow after centuries of being chosen to provide the Word in a new and improved religion, prosperity preachers' flocks are mostly missing or not getting the message. Changes just for the sake of change do not equate growth in Christ. If what Christ provided over two thousand years ago was perfect, why all the improvements? Perhaps forgiveness is in order to all the visionaries throughout the centuries who sought to improve the Word, because they know not what they do.

First Amendment Intolerance

Everyone seems to know when others are being intolerant to their interests, but not everyone knows when they are intolerant to the interests of others. Some believe particular interests should have higher consideration than others, and if others submitted to that lower position, there would not be a problem. The problem comes when those conflicting interests expect equal footing or consideration just because it says so in the constitution.

Take religious freedom for instance. Since Judeo-Christian is believed to be the original settlers' religion of choice, all latecomers should take their rightful back seat or subordinate place. Although the initial settlers, Native Americans, had a belief, it was thought to be too salvage or barbaric to the trespassers (Christians). Those who differed are automatically assigned anti-Christian or anti-American titles. The thinking is, there is no way the ones who hold different beliefs can give the Christian faith its due respect if they select another religion. One picking an alternate choice is rejecting Christianity. It's putting another God above the God of Christianity. The reason Christians know this is that it is anti-Christian to profess anything that is lukewarm or counter to the teachings of Christ.

Election of Christianity means rejecting acknowledgment and sometimes even the right for other religions to exist. All other religions are inferior to the original. They should be granted First Amendment protections in words only. Now Christians may not state it that bluntly because of the First Amendment, but their fight for religious rights is all about Christian rights, and their thinking is that Christian rights are superior to First Amendment rights. Some believe the founding fathers never meant to include other faiths. The proof of that is the dismissive approach they took with the Native-American and African-American religions at the time. However, many of the founding fathers were nonreligious.

How can one hold to one faith while respecting and allowing another to worship in an entirely different manner and not feel as if such toleration subtracts or infringes on the beliefs one holds? The growth of religions is on how convincing one can demonstrate uniqueness. There is a fear that granting another equal footing means a lowering of the individual's belief. Christianity without its level of awe is just another religion.

One could argue that Christianity, from the beginning, bene-fited from exclusiveness and favor. Because of that head start, it has been assigned a superiority position in the minds of many. Although it has endured persecutions and distortions in many circles as other religions have, a lot of that has come from within Christianity. It has resulted in splits and different sects.

The American Constitution puts religious freedom in writing as a First Amendment right. The American people, through toler-ance, must guarantee that expression no matter how opposed. That is the only way to maintain the very freedoms the founders intended because of the religious persecutions from which they were fleeing.

It is religious intolerance around the world that contributes to the many unspeakable horrors surrounding world religions. That is true in Islam, as displayed by the actions of the Sunnis and Shiites, and in Israel, where the Palestinians and Jews have been feuding for centuries. Intolerance opens the door to behaviors that, in the minds of some, conclude it is okay to use violence to eradicate perceived slights of their God or religion. At the root of all this is the belief that permitting religious disrespect or slights leads to spiritual destruction.

All must share in the toleration and protection of religion. Christianity also deserves tolerance in America and around the world even if it is the dominant religion in America. Tolerance revered unequally is a form of limited understanding that amounts to intolerance. The justification of religious intolerance is always explained away along religious lines.

The belief is that if any religion accepts a different belief, then they are all equal, even one that rejects eternal life. Some believe that such similar acceptance will render Christianity less significant and, in time, irrelevant. Religious paranoia warns of a domino effect much like the communist fervor that existed during the Vietnam era. It keeps religions at war with one another. The proof of this is evident by centuries of religious strife and discourse. It is doubtful it will end anytime soon.

Religious intolerance amounts to religious segregation that is no different from education segregation. Martin Luther King Jr. once called eleven o'clock at Sunday morning as the most segregated hour in America. Religious teaching is an education along a religious line that will culminate into religious superiority thinking, which will lead to discriminatory practices no different from other forms of discrimination. Not being able to locally coexist religiously threatens not just religious existence globally but also all humanity's existence.

The Golden Rule exists in some form or another in almost every major religion, and almost all of them are centuries older than Christianity. The thinking that it originated in Christianity is just one entrenched falsehood perpetrated as proof of Christians' superiority.

In my view, intolerance and bias toward different religions are to be acknowledged, recognized, and honestly addressed with respect to the First Amendment guarantee. To do otherwise is hypocritical. It undermines the core Judeo-Christian principles and values professed by Christians on which this country stands.

HOWARD CALHOUN

Politics and Religions

Most of us have heard I never discuss religion or politics with so and so. The why is interesting but not very reasonable. I have heard it is the fastest way to lose a friend or a family member. So, is the political or religious affiliation more important than the friend or the family member? Why is holding a different politics or religion a condition of a friendship or a family relationship? What is it about someone belonging to a different religion or politics that makes it impossible for friends or family members to coexist after communicating along religious or political lines? I have known friends and family members to come to blows over religion or politics. Thank God, the age of duels in politics (eighteenth to late nineteenth centuries) has passed us. In a country that prides itself on freedom, the only freedom that can exist is defined by the last one standing.

Religion and politics are two issues that make people less smart. I do not mean being affiliated with a certain religion or a certain politics makes one less sharp because it is not the religion or the politics that matters. When someone defends a religion or politics, the person insists on holding steadfast the views of whatever religion or politics one follows. That loyalty makes people unable to listen and think outside whatever position they hold. There is nothing reasonable if it differs from one's politics or religion. That is why I say religion and politics make one less bright. Christianity's history and relationship to the facilitation and maintenance of slavery and Jim Crow laws are always glossed over as if there is no connection. When one is unwilling to think or listen to rationality because of a politics' or religion's position, it is hard to reason how that person is getting smarter or how it is better for our country. Often intransigence is viewed as intelligence when one is perceived to be judged by an identified enemy.

I have been told I was born a Christian and a democrat and I am going to die a Christian and a democrat. Neither of these is a natural condition of birth. A free country affords a person the right to hold those positions and legislate their defense. I will join those defending the right to hold the positions, but it may not be the most reasonable thing to do or confess if the positions have not been examined

140

since birth. I have heard the statement, "I am such and such because my family has always been republicans or Catholics." I do not know why that makes sense or why someone would follow it like it is the most sensible thing about the whole family. I have heard, "I will vote for a Russian before I will vote for a democrat" and "I would rather be dead than vote for a republican, really." "I do not see how he or she can be a Mormon or a Muslim." Often we casually point out the insufficiency in others' religions and politics but cannot see or acknowledge areas of deficiencies in ours.

It leads me to my answer to why people do not discuss religion or politics. When anal-thinking people are taking rigid positions into communication, it is a double whammy. It does not matter if it is a family member or a friend. It is two loggerheads who cannot think beyond their positions due to some long-standing loyalty or custom with a questionable or untraceable origin. If one is unable to acknowledge a reasonable toleration for the religion position of a friend or family member, it is best not discuss religion or politics, but oh, how much smarter one could become if one learns the many religions and politics of all those of which one disagrees and the reasons why the beliefs are so sacred.

Godspeed

The notion that those who are inspired by God are perfect and are incapable of constructing a document without imperfections at least deserves a critical look.

Now imagine being asked to contribute 10 percent or more of your income to a business venture yet not be allowed to question. Committing 10 percent or more of your salary on a regular basis to anything without questions would be viewed as foolish by general standards. However, to contribute 10 percent of a salary and then have someone tell you that "As God's shepherd, I am entitled to see an income statement to make sure God is getting all his money" without question seems beyond the pale.

Those standing in for God say they are only messengers and extensions of God's Word. They have been inspired, called, or chosen and really should not have to answer about doing God's work and should only have to answer to God. As one listens to the chosen one speak of what God is entitled, what are you afforded from God through his vessel for your 10 percent? Would you not get the same without his chosen one provided you provided 10 percent through some other medium, seeing that the gift comes from God and since God is everywhere? Are you allowed to raise questions about expectations and with whom or if this a down payment on salvation? We have had that argument many times before, most noticeably, with "Luther's 95 Theses."

If it is not an investment in salvation, what is it an investment in, or why should I not refer to it as an investment, especially since it appears to be a recurring weekly or monthly expense on something? If I am not allowed to question, to me, there seems to be something amiss. An unquestionable arrangement involving a potentially unlimited and steady supply of funds would probably even tempt the godly inspired.

Over time, one may not be able to tell the difference. Since this arrangement plays on people's internal and external fears on this earth and their domestic and eternal hopes and aspirations beyond this planet, they are strangely trapped, so barring a viable alternative, what gives?

Another troubling observation about this investment is the easy access to becoming stewards of this venture. You merely must be inspired, called, chosen, or whatever the term one wishes to use. So if God has requested my services, then who among you are high enough to question God? It invites those unskilled and unqualified for anything else to step forward. It is also an opportunity to be revered by society without having to train, educate, or seek credentials usually required by other professions.

Because of the potential windfall versus minimum risk or output, there is a prospect to purchase an even higher standing than the one chosen or called. In the end, money talks. Chosen ones are hardly infallible; therefore, questioning a chosen one may be as necessary as the shepherd calling the sheep to order.

Man's Waterloo

I think humanity erred in institutionalizing and capitalizing religion. Some things should remain sacred and stay protected from the impulses and the cunning mind of man. As great of an idea as it was for the founding fathers of America to finally settle on separating state from religion, I think it would have served humankind better had they went a little further and kept religion safe from the influences of money and institutional prejudices and biases. The decision not to exclude religion makes us witnesses and perpetrators to one of the first and greatest sins.

Those who championed no tax on God's work also advocated a big payoff with little or no oversight; an unlimited money machine with the task of policing itself in a capitalistic system is a dream. Surely no one would misuse God's money.

For prosperity religions and prosperity preachers, money, power, and influence shield them from ever knowing real prosperity. It allows opportunities for them to redefine success on their terms and promote individual interpretations to their members. Members who are in lockstep with their preachers will not see themselves as being misled or as enablers.

Prosperity preachers have become celebrities within the megachurch movement. The trendsetters are spurring dissatisfaction and upheaval in smaller churches. The place and the leaders are the focus instead of the spiritual needs of the parishioners. With twenty thousand or more members, stewardship requires multiple assistants.

Religious leaders blinded by their fame and auditory skills lose empathy for those who contribute to their wealth and prosperity. Worshippers brag to others about being in attendance with a famous preacher as if that has value. Programs about the renowned preacher and even preachers' wives are making their way across the landscape, in the name of God and man-made reality television. The love of money is the issue, but lines are too blurred to tell the difference. If religion is the institution responsible for setting the moral course of society, this new age wave is crying out, "Who is going to save us from ourselves?"

Members have become enthralled by the fame of their leaders. One minister complained of having to take out a restraining order of protection against female worshippers. Ministers are falling in love with their glory. Religious conferences are opportunities for ministers to show off their newfound wealth, fraternize, and womanize. Those with lesser wealth who lost the race take smaller roles in church business and leadership and find fame and fortune as understudies. Ministers opposed to the "bigger is better" phenomenon are yielding to "if you can't beat them, join them."

One church member told me that his church allows members to borrow money at 25 percent interest, but he said, "It was cheaper to borrow from me." I know religion is business. Are there any lines not crossable? Should pastors lend members their own money at such high-interest rate? I thought the church provided for those in need, not profited from those in need. Where there is greed, there is no grace.

The money amassed by the religious institution makes it one of the most influential institutions in society. It influences politics and other entities in society more due to its wealth than its moral positions. Money not only influences but also corrupts. Many times, they throw their block support behind political candidate's counter to their morals if it means more money and profits for their coffers. Evangelicals and others accused of selling out morally are unmoved when faced with the truth if it conflicts with political or economic preference.

There is nothing wrong with an institution designed for capitalization to make money, but when an organization intended to save man from himself and the evils of the world gets tangled in the very things it is supposed to protect man from, eventually it becomes too tainted and corrupt to deliver reliable spiritual messages. Those who critique the choices and directions of a religious leader or the religious institutions are subject to a raft that is not very spiritual.

The United States is said to be a Judeo-Christian settlement whether we like it or not. Exercising one's freedom of religion counter to the state's original selection or assignment can be painful and unsettling based on who is interpreting. It makes one wonder if such democracy is merely a submission to society's pressure to avoid social and economic pains.

Cassius Clay used his religious freedom and right to become a Muslim after he won the heavyweight boxing championship. His title gets taken for exercising his religious rights. Numerous Judeo-Christian ministers protested his freedom of choice as if it was somehow out of step to their religious choice. Pres. Barrack Obama got a lot of grief because of his Muslim-sounding name. Had he implored his First Amendment right to become a Muslim, respecting his decision would probably turn into an impeachment hearing.

If the founders' original goal was to keep religion free and sacred from the dictates of the state and religious mob bosses, then leaving it to the conscience of individuals as if the Holy Spirit would cleanse the influences of money and the biases were fantasy thinking.

Much of this described may have taken place even without the founding fathers excluding church and church business from the seedy side of capitalism. Not separating it made it a certainty. The trend is sure to get worse. Greed and misappropriation of money and power are spreading faster than spirituality. This direction should be concerning to those responsible for the integrity of this great institution. Accusations of sexual improprieties and exploitation, money laundering, and a host of other dishonorable mentions are being pushed under the rug for the sake of image and more money. Cancer does eat itself from the inside.

Just raising the possibility of possible improprieties within such a powerful institution is viewed as blasphemy. I am sure that biting the hand that feeds is right in this instance. This institution is way too big to fail. And it indeed should not, but this does not mean it should not be reined in. Is it trying to make necessary corrections? To expect a severely critical review and a meaningful overhaul by those invested is to expect fortunes to become unpopular. What will it matter at the end of the day? The love of money has caused the church and other religious institutions to lose sight of their mission: what really matters at the end of day. The founding fathers were not prophets. Apparently, they did not see this coming. Lord only knows where it will end.

No Ordinary Citizen

I stop by to tell you that you are a product of God. You were meant to be celebrated just by this one statement: "Greater is he that is in you than he that is in the world." But then something happened to you that separated you from that greatness.

What happens to a person means someone else does something to another person that influences that person against his will or intent. Too often that becomes the deciding factor in what another person becomes. The outcome can be damaging when another person decides to do harm to another. A person with malice in his heart toward another person is not going to make sure the other person becomes the best he can be. That is where "greater is he that is in me than he that is in the world" comes into play. Whatever happens to you is never more significant than what is within you. Lean not unto your understanding when it comes to this one.

When someone does something to another for his benefit, it is usually just that—for his interest. That is an eternal truth. The things we focus on are the things we attract. If we focus on the negative things that happen to us, we invite the negative forces and the power that come with it. Focus on what you want to attract. Knowing what is within you is a power to call on to magnify what you want to become. By choosing to focus on that greatness within, it naturally negates the strength of all the negatives. No weapon formed against you shall prosper.

The lemons become lemonade. Barriers become projectiles. Stumbling blocks become launching pads. "Greater is he that is in you" turns every mountain you face into a molehill, and God's destiny is revealed to you. The things that were supposed to beat you down become appetizers that strengthen you. "I will never leave nor forsake you." The worst slave master of all time cannot defeat the God in you. There is no more accurate statement than, "Greater is he that is in me than he that is in the world." The Conqueror of all times lives within you. God is at least one trillion to zero. He is undefeated. You are undefeatable. You are the end product of generations of conquerors. You, with the he in you, are no ordinary citizen.

God's Gift

What is a blessing? People wish for more height, more intellect, more beauty, more talent, more charm, more riches, a boy, a husband, and on and on. I listen to more pity parties from more folks about how God passed them. I wonder if the air they breathe is not from somewhere else or tainted in some way. How is it that many can find time to complain without noticing the power to be able to complain as a blessing? Do we think the capacity to speak is a given and not know there are many who no longer have that ability and would trade places with us in a skinny minute? If one is unable to recognize and utilize current blessings, where is the evidence that one would not squander more blessings?

What I am referring to are neither foreign concepts nor original notions. What I speak of is old, pure, and in the same vein as, "I cried because I had no shoes until I met a man who had no feet" and "You don't miss your water until your well runs dry." So why are so many still mystified by God's gift?

We whine about what we do not have to the exclusion of what we do have. Whatever God has in store for us or whatever we were destined to become is within our creation. To seek or to expect to create something different or better that is separate from what God created us to be is to repute God. Like the credo, "Ford has a better idea," we have a better idea.

We do not make improvements on what God has created without making a mess. Many never become close to what they were destined to become due to too many off-road glances. Glances become stares blocking God's harmony and blessing.

For years, I nearly fell into that same trap as I sought high and low for the sense and meaning in my stuttering. My attempts at a cure always seemed to fall short. I felt I was passed over just because my speech failed me in critical moments. Although I knew and I knew they knew there were laws against discrimination, there were always other useful ploys employers and others could use in denouncing me, primarily since sometimes I was unable to complete a sentence. They could say I failed to provide them with clear answers. I felt cursed. Nothing good would ever become of me due to my stuttering. Since God provided it, I thought I was destined to damnation. I could never amount to anything. That was God's promise to me, so I might as well get used to it and stop fighting. Little did I know by not fighting, I was yielding to God's will and aligning myself with the harmony and destiny of God. I was able to learn that God does not give anything but gifts, so if it came with my creation, it must be good. It has a purpose. It is up to me to understand that it is a gift and it has a meaning, and now that I can receive that blessing as the blessing it is, I must be about the business of finding out just how much of a benefit it is.

My most significant disadvantage, which was never a disadvantage at all, is now my greatest advantage. My willingness to accept my stuttering strips many fluent speakers of their rationale to not speak and offers the most excellent motivation for me to speak all while offering inspiration to those most reluctant to talk. My creation was as foretold. My purpose and destiny are one. I and all I have or will become is God's gift.

My Final Thoughts

I think most have heard that everything happens for a reason. As one of the subscribers, I wish to share my thinking in search of that reason. Why are some folks willing to risk our democratic system to an autocratic system? In a democratic system, equality is the goal, but the greater number in one group will make it the majority and dominate class. Whatever that group decides is fair in the democratic process. It produces good days for that group. Little thought is given to the kind of days it creates for those with less votes. Why all the complaining? It is the democratic process at work. Never mind. At one time, the minority did not get a chance to vote. That was determined by the democratic majority. The majority is supposed to decide in a democracy but maintain acknowledgment of the minority. As the demographic changes and the reality shifts the majority into the minority, it enlightens the majority to the plight of the minority, and suddenly the good old days are receding or, shall I say, trending to a different group. As this becomes clearer, the emerging of a new or different good old days is looming.

I do not mean to simplify or make light of this matter. It is a big deal. It affects every facet of life, including traditions, lifestyle, culture, economics, and language. I think there is a segment of the white race where privilege has been of little benefit. Reconciling the favorite status of being white while being an underprivileged component of the white majority will be tricky when maintaining the benefit of white becomes less than qualifying as a new minority as long as that minority is not confused with the black and brown. Life will change forever for the new and old majority, but our greatness has been spurred by acclimation and adaptation. Probably the biggest and most important change will be the gradual shift in power. Being in power for centuries is seen as an earned position that should not be confused with privilege. It certainly should not be given up because of a change in numbers. Race is what makes an American. Whites understand that better than anyone because not too long ago, Irish, Italians, Greeks, Germans, Jewish, and many others came to this country as ethnic groups. They were rejected as immigrants but were willing to abdicate ethnocentricity in favor of the superiority and privileged status of becoming "white" Americans. Once integrated, lost on them, is what it was like to be shunned. It is the giving up or the sharing of power that some cannot accept. That brings me back to the question of why some are willing to risk a democratic system for an autocratic system.

Rather than accept or share an equal or subordinate position in a democratic system, it is better to changeover to an autocratic system where the power can stay the same and who matters will remain the same. Make no mistake about this: power will not be conceded without a fight. They know that once in power as an autocrat, numbers will not matter, no rules will apply to them, and they will be able to do as they please with no fear of repercussion. Once out of power, the grappling to ensure white lives matter may be untenable given its history of repression and oppression to ensure black lives never mattered. Yes, it is time to dismiss with the democratic experience. Is the sharing of power too much to ask?

Russia has a 616-member parliament, which consists of a lower and upper house called the federal assembly. Russia has 115 members of the Supreme Court, nominated by the president and appointed by the federation council. Who among these would accuse Putin of a crime, and who would be bold enough to try to convict him? It does not matter how many other bodies of government you have if autocracy is the system of governance. When democracy no longer serves the interest of those in power, those in power will look for power by any means necessary. There is absolutely nothing they will not do to stay in power. Our republic is at stake. Those enablers thinking it may be better to live under an autocracy as a minority than live under a democracy as a minority must understand that autocratic power and the good old days, which will follow, will rest and reside only with those in power. To ensure no threat to their power, the Second Amendment may very well be the First Amendment that goes. To keep this democracy is an honored burden.

About the Author

H oward Calhoun is the author of *In the Shadow of Sacrifice*. He is a licensed clinical mental health counselor supervisor, a licensed addiction counselor supervisor, a licensed school counselor, and a licensed real estate broker. He is an owner and CEO of a mental health and substance abuse agency that serves North and South Carolina. He is the president and owner of a real estate venture with his brother and owner of a nonprofit education and scholarship business, TESS of North Carolina, that includes a Rosenwald school. He enjoys motivational speaking. His encouragement to others is to make learning synonymous with breathing. His favorite motto is, "Childhood is but for one reason: preparation for adulthood."

CPSIA information can be obtained
at www.ICGtesting.com
Printed in the USA
BVHW080604300321
603653BV00005B/794